MISHPOCHAH

the Jewish way to say family

MATTERS

SPEAKING FRANKLY
TO GOD'S FAMILY

David Brickner

Purple Pomegranate Productions
San Francisco, California

Acknowledgments

I want to thank my editor, Ruth Rosen. We have been friends since childhood, but friendship is best enjoyed when people serve together. That proved to be the case throughout the five years that we co-labored over these and other *Mishpochah Messages.* Ruth is a sensitive writer and an incisive thinker who loves God and His Word. She invariably sharpens and clarifies my ideas and has contributed significantly to this project.

—David Brickner

Cover Design by Sue Saunders

© Copyright 1996, Purple Pomegranate Productions
All essays except the author's afterword were previously published by Jews for Jesus in the Mishpochah Message, a quarterly publication for Jewish believers in Jesus.

96 97 98 98 00 10 9 8 7 6 5 4 3 2 1

Brickner, David N. 1958-
Mishpochah Matters/by David N. Brickner—1st ed.

Library of Congress Cataloging-Publication Data
Mishpochah Matters
     p.   cm.
  ISBN: 1-881022-24-2 (pbk.)
  1. Jewish Christians—Religious life. 2. Christian life.
BR158.M57 1996
289.9—dc20   96-30755
                              CIP

Contents

A Guide to This Anthology

It is fitting to begin this collection with a couple of essays dealing with fundamentals of Christian life. In Part One, "Walking With God," David Brickner offers important advice from a Jewish Christian vantage point on questions that some might not think to ask their own pastors: how do we distinguish God's leading from our own ambitions? What practical guidelines can help us live a life pleasing to the Savior? What does it mean to take up our cross and follow Him?

Part Two, "Walking With God's Family," is the longest because in the community of Jewish believers (and perhaps in the larger body of Christ as well), these are issues people find most difficult to discuss with their pastors. How can Jewish believers fit in as a minority in the local church? How should one handle feelings of cultural alienation among brothers and sisters in Christ? How can we appreciate our differences without causing division? What should one look for in a pastor? What about Messianic congregations?[1]

Part Three, "Walking Through the Seasons of Life," deals directly with such intimate matters as our choices regarding marriage and the process fo aging. How should we view the option of celibacy as opposed to marriage? If we marry, what considerations are important for the Jewish believer in Jesus? How are we to face the challenge of growing older for our loved ones and ourselves? How can we confront the issue of death in a way that will glorify the risen Lord?

Part Four, "Walking Through (Not Around) Tough Issues," takes readers through some weighty matters: "Symbols and Substance" will immediately captivate the person who is interested in philosophy. It is a multifaceted gem well worth mining. Also in this section, Brickner addresses questions that tend to be focal points of debate among Christians: how should we regard miracles? What should we expect concerning Christ's return?

---

1. Congregations of Jewish and Gentile believers in Jesus who worship in a Jewish way.

Finally, in an author's afterword, Brickner stresses what every Christian needs to know regarding the most urgent need of Jewish people today. This article draws the other essays into perspective as the reader considers how the Lord would have Christians relate not just to believing Jews but also to unbelieving Jewish people today.

Preface

Jews who come to Christ face many challenges. Where shall they go? What shall they do? How can they deal with family? Where should they compromise? When should they take a stand? How can they know the will of God? Questions, questions, questions, and sometimes the unique circumstances of a Jewish believer put the pastor of a conventional church at a loss for answers.

David Brickner served as Jews for Jesus' minister-at-large for five years and dealt with the problems of Jewish believers. These essays are samplings of his teaching, and if they remind you of two New Testament books, James and Hebrews, you are right on point.

Though the essays were originally written to Jewish Christians, I think they will speak to everyone. After all, James and Hebrews were written to Jewish believers, and they have been a blessing to the Church. And so the Jews for Jesus organization passes these on to you—not as the inerrant Word of God, but as helpful commentary on modern times and how to keep focused on the God of all ages.

David Brickner is a dynamic young man who leads through example. He grew up in a Jewish Christian home, and from his childhood he has had a knowledge of the Lord and of Scriptures. He has ministered from pulpits all over the world, but his special ministry has been to lead and guide those Jewish believers in Jesus who were seeking to follow the Lord more closely. Though he is relatively young, he writes like the church fathers, as a person with intrinsic authority on those subjects he chooses to address.

Brickner, now the executive director of Jews for Jesus, is a mission leader with a pastor's heart. He is able to embrace individuals and encourage them to trust more and to go further into to the One who says, "I am the Way, the Truth and the Life."

Moishe Rosen, founder
Jews for Jesus

Foreword

There's an old Yiddish proverb that goes like this: "*Got hot zikh bashafn a velt mit kleyne veltelekh.*"[1] In English: God created a world full of little worlds.

I'd like to welcome you into one of the little worlds God has created.

The community of Jews who believe in Jesus is small but vibrant and growing stronger all the time. We know that when it comes to our standing before God, there is neither Jew nor Greek, male nor female. But when we stand beside one another, we recognize that some of us are male and others are female, some are Jewish, others are not. God did not limit the human race to one earthly culture and heritage any more than He limited us to one gender. Differences should not divide us; on the contrary, they can be a source of wonder and joy, especially if we take them into account as we serve one another.

During my tenure as Jews for Jesus' minister-at-large, I had the privilege of ministering to the community of Jewish Christians through a publication called the *Mishpochah Message* (mishpochah is the Jewish way to say family).[2] This book is a compilation of some of those messages.

We hope a glimpse into our little world will fascinate and enrich the larger body of Christ—because the Jewish people have always been a microcosm of the larger society. Leo Rosten, author of *The Joys of Yiddish,* put it this way, "Jewish people are just like everyone else—only more so!"

If you are a Jewish believer in Jesus, these messages should not need much introduction—they were originally written for you. And if you are not Jewish, don't worry, you won't be

---

1. Hanan J. Ayalti, ed., *Yiddish Proverbs* (New York: Schocken Books, 1949), pp. 80-81.

2. The *Yiddish pronunciation* of mishpochah *puts the accent on the second syllable. The "o" is pronounced like the "u" in the word* put. *The "ch" is not pronounced like* chat; *it's a softer sound made with the back of the tongue against the soft palate. The easiest way to do it, you'll excuse me, is by clearing your throat. If that doesn't work, just pronounce the "c" without the "h."*

eavesdropping. In fact, I am especially eager for you to read on because this is an opportunity for you to see a bit of our little world. Some of the frank observations and comments may surprise you. I'll address a few issues and challenges that you probably have not faced—but mostly you will encounter issues, challenges, and more important you will encounter principles that pertain to all believers in Jesus, whether Jew or Gentile. Perhaps seeing them in a different context will shed a bit of new light on the old truths we may sometimes take for granted.

As you read, I hope you will be encouraged. I hope you will find that the concerns of Jewish believers are not so different from your own. We are united in Him: we have the same Heavenly Father, the same Savior, the same Spirit. Moreover, we have the same Scriptures, the same mandate for godly living and the same eternal destiny! So pull up a chair, take off your shoes and get comfortable . . . you're with mishpochah.

David Brickner, executive director
Jews for Jesus

To my father, Avi Brickner, who always speaks best when he writes. By his example he has taught me to love writing. He hasn't written as much as I think he should, but perhaps that is because he knows that words should be weighed, not counted. I am blessed by the weighty inheritance he has given me.

Part One
Walking With God

Are You Called?

The voice startled him into wakeful alertness. He sat up on the edge of the bed. "Did someone call?" Silence. Perhaps it was a dream, though if it was he had dreamed it for the second time that night. Perhaps he should inquire of his mentor, but the bed was warm against the chill of night air, and its comfort beckoned him with the promise of a few more hours of sleep. Just as he had burrowed back down beneath the blanket, he heard the voice again. This time it was more insistent. He must get up. He must go. He must answer the call. Soon he would discover that the voice was not the voice of an ordinary mentor or friend. It was the voice of the Holy One of Israel summoning Samuel to serve.

Few of us have had, or can expect to have, as dramatic a calling as young Samuel. Many have sensed God's calling with as much certainty through far more ordinary events, while others wish we could reassure ourselves with the memory of an audible voice telling us God's specific will for our lives. We wonder, "How would I know if I were called? How can I discover if God is calling me?" Some who were once certain find themselves wondering, "Have I *really* been called?"

The world is filled with voices that continually call out to us, beckoning us to choose a certain path, or urging us to join a particular cause. Some voices soothe us into self-indulgence while others call us to involve ourselves in noble endeavors. Either way, the din of voices can confuse us. For some, it might even drown out that still, small voice that may be calling our name. The heart speaks loudly, confidently and reassuringly when it is leading us to deceive ourselves.

As followers of Y'shua (Jesus) and members of the mishpochah, we need to sort out the voices and develop ears to recognize that still, small voice so that we may know when God is calling.

The Scriptures give ample information concerning God's call. God clearly calls everyone to recognize who He is. Psalm 19 describes how He does this in two ways. First, God reveals Himself in a general way through His creation. "The heavens declare the glory of God; and the firmament shows His handiwork" (verse 1). God also beckons us in a specific way through the revelation of His written Word. Scriptures speak to our hearts, "converting the soul" (verse 7).

How gracious our God is to speak to us both in the wonders of His creation and in His wonderful Word. However, this calling and evidence of God's grace does not ensure an answer. God is willing that none shall perish (2 Peter 3:9). Many are called, but few are chosen (Matthew 22:14). Our sovereign God allows human beings free will, and some choose not to come when He calls. God's calling is a great mystery. Those who receive His *effectual* call—the call that leads to salvation—have a real choice, and yet salvation is just as much a product of His gracious choosing. "Moreover whom He predestined, these He also called; whom He called, these He also justified; and whom He justified, these He also glorified" (Romans 8:30).

God's general calling to all people includes a presentation of the facts of the gospel and an offering of salvation with an earnest exhortation to accept God's grace. The effectual call provides the moral persuasion and the power of the Holy Spirit to effect new life and new birth. It leads to redemption and salvation in the Messiah. All blood-bought, heaven-born believers have experienced this calling.

In calling us to salvation, God did much more than grant us a fire insurance policy to snatch us from hell. Salvation is a complex gift, consisting of more than one good. In fact, it is a bundle of benefits. Many people use the word *salvation* to refer to one part of that bundle: justification. When we trust Jesus as our Messiah, we are made just in God's eyes; God imputes Y'shua's righteousness to us and writes us into His book of life. It is justification that rescues us from the jaws of eternal death and destines us to be with God forever.

When God saved us, He not only justified us, but He also called us to be sanctified, and He called us to serve. Each one of God's children is called to be a living example of His grace in the world today. When God saved us, He extended to us a whole new way of living, thinking and being that leads us to become like Y'shua. All believers and followers of Y'shua are called to be renewed and transformed.

It is a high or *upward* calling in which God's standards for what we do, say and even think require us to rise above what the world considers acceptable. It is a holy calling. We are to be separated out from others who have not heeded the call. That does not mean that we should ostracize nonbelievers. Yet we are called to be different from those who do not follow the One who called us. We have a heavenly calling, a destiny far above and beyond this world and its limitations. As God called our ancestors out of Egypt, He calls us to be free from all that would hinder us from belonging to Him. As believers in Jesus, we experience a measure of that freedom here, but we are ultimately destined for a place where nothing will impede our dedication to God.

Some believers in Jesus receive a further call to God's "special service." That call might be manifested supernaturally. Those who are sensitive and tuned in to the Lord's leading might hear an audible voice as Samuel did. They might receive something so profoundly personal that it is just as clear as an audible voice. But God sometimes intervenes in the lives of those who are not tuned in to His will and His ways. Like Saul of Tarsus, some of us had our minds and hearts set on something other than what God wanted until He knocked us off our horse with a blinding light to get our attention.

Still other people think God might be calling them to a certain kind of ministry, but they are not certain. I often speak to people who wonder how they can know whether they are being called by God for special service.

It is easy to elevate our own plans—especially if they are noble and God honoring—to attribute a higher status to them and to believe that our plans are God's plans. The problem is, if those plans do not come to fruition, we tend to be angry with God or angry with the people we expected to help us follow what we thought was God's call.

On the other hand, what if this thing we find ourselves preoccupied with doing really is God's call? If we ignore it, or if we are afraid to give ourselves to the task, for how much less will our lives count? What glorious crowns that we might have presented to the King will be discarded by the wayside?

It's serious business to be able to discern the difference between our own inclinations and God's call. There are several indications to help people discern such a calling.

Realistic Assessment of Your Own Will

It is important to discern your own will if you want to be able to know God's will. We all have dreams, desires, goals and ambitions. People who piously insist that they have no will other than to do God's will have deceived themselves and can easily mistake their own will for God's will. That is not to say that God's will is always diametrically opposed to our own. But once you admit that something is your will, you can be pleasantly surprised if you find that it seems to be God's will as well.

The Scriptures tell us to delight ourselves in the Lord and He will give us the desires of our hearts. Some people selfishly interpret this as a promise that if we get the hang of delighting ourselves in the Lord—whatever that means—we will have whatever we desire, be that material possessions, a spouse, children or a particular position in our chosen vocation.

In reality, delighting ourselves in the Lord has a direct bearing on our desires. When His delight becomes our desire, when His Kingdom becomes our calling, when His desires become our privilege to fulfill, then His will and our will are in harmony, and we have the confidence of His call.

A Compelling Desire to Do for God

When a person is called, he or she becomes conscious of a compelling desire, even need, to do something for God. Often our most compelling desires are to do for ourselves, for our mates or for our children. But a burning desire to do something for God might be an indication of calling. The Apostle Paul said, "Woe is me if I do not preach the gospel" (1 Corinthians 9:16). John Knox said to the Lord, "Give me Scotland ere I die." If you are called, you will feel an overpowering burden that something must be done and must be done by you, a feeling that you will explode if you do not loose your energy for the doing of this task. Such a calling is a wonderful merging of God's wooing and our own desires.

A Confirmation in the Community of Believers

A second indication of your call is when others testify that you are intellectually as well as spiritually qualified to serve in a particular way. Brothers and sisters in Israel have lamented (and I can empathize with them) over some who have come to Israel because they felt God had called them there to minister—yet they had no idea of what life is like in Israel. Some have remained in the land with little or no knowledge of Hebrew, the heart language of the people they want to reach. They seem as confident as ever that God has called them, though there is no indication that ministry is taking place, and there is no one who can confirm the calling.

On the other hand, confirmation does not always come when we would like it to, nor does it necessarily come from whom we might expect it. For example, Gladys Aylward was turned down by the China Inland Mission at the age of twenty-six. She had done quite poorly on her theology exam and was considered academically deficient. She was also considered too old to learn all that was necessary for the field. Yet she had an all-consuming desire to get to China. She spent everything, risked her life to get there—and was used by God in a mighty way. The people whom she led to faith and those who worked by her side confirmed God's call in her life. Perhaps it was necessary for Gladys Aylward to be rejected by the China Inland Mission in order for her to fulfill her destiny.

A person's calling may or may not be obvious to others from the start. But if someone is called by God, he or she will be used by God. And if someone is used by God, *there will be others who can confirm it.* God's call is not issued into a vacuum. It echoes; it resonates in the hearts of others.

If you believe that God is calling you to ministry, be willing to subject yourself to self-examination as well as the scrutiny of others who have experience in ministry. Allow the collective wisdom of those whom God has placed in your life to be further guidance for you.

Objective Tests of Truth

There are three tests of truth that we can reasonably apply to the question, "How can I know that I am called?"

The first test of truth is *pragmatic.* Does it work? For example, if you feel that God has called you to be an evangelist, a fair question to ask is, "Have you led anyone to the Lord?" If God is calling you to evangelism, there should be some visible demonstration of that calling in your life and of the gifts that are necessary to the office of evangelist.

If your calling involves travel and a major transition, be willing to test it where you are before you actually go. Returning to an earlier example, many people have told me that God has called them to reach our people in Israel. I usually ask what they are doing to reach our people where they are. Some are offended by the question, but usually not those who are involved or willing to involve themselves in Jewish evangelism. After all, why wouldn't those who are called to reach out to Jewish people in Israel make the effort to reach out to the Jewish people in their own community? Does anyone think it is easier to take a stand for the gospel in Israel?

If you feel called to be an evangelist but have never led anyone to the Lord because you don't know how, there are short-term evangelistic programs whereby you can receive both training and opportunities to test your calling. Be selective. Many worthwhile projects, such as building homes or churches, may not provide training and opportunities for you to lead a person to Christ. Many things that fall under the label of "missions" actually entail little if any personal evangelism.

At Jews for Jesus, we encourage people who are interested in serving with us to try a short-term mission project such as our annual Summer Witnessing Campaign. I often tell people it is like dating before getting engaged. Short-term ministry allows you to experience what it is like to serve the Lord. It can be a reality check. Romanticizing ministry only leads to disappointment, but sharing in the joys as well as hardships can lead to a well-balanced and informed decision.

The second test is that of *cohesion.* Does it fit together? To overstate an example, let's say that an individual is convinced that God has called him to serve in another country, but he is enlisted for a three-year term in the military. He can only answer such a "call" if he goes AWOL from the military. The profession of calling has no cohesion because it doesn't fit together with the other facts of the person's life. God does not call people to dishonor their commitments.

The third test of truth is *correspondence.* Does what I say God has called me to do correspond with reality? For example, if I say God has called me to write, direct and act in a screenplay that will attract secular audiences to the gospel, many facts must correspond. Who, besides me, finds my screenplay worthy of production? What will draw unbelieving audiences to this movie? Who believes I am a good actor? What other talented actors and actresses will take my direction? How will I pay for this project to be completed and publicized? The answers to all of these questions must correspond to reality and to what I say my calling is and what I am capable of doing or producing.

God's Provision

God always provides the means for us to answer His call. That is not to say that God makes it easy for us to obey Him. More often than not, it will be the opposite. For example, if you are a schoolteacher and you believe God is calling you into ministry, you might find it suddenly becomes very comfortable and secure for you to stay where you are. Perhaps you will receive a big raise, more academic freedom, the outstanding teacher of the year award. In other words, if you believe God is calling you, do not be surprised if you are offered all kinds of blandishments for *not* doing what God is calling you to do.

It's easy to view worldly incentives as God-given opportunities, either to continue on a present course or to take a different direction from the one that God had seemed to indicate. God certainly uses many circumstances to bless and encourage us. But if God is calling you, "blessings" might actually be obstacles. More obvious obstacles might also crop up, such as difficulty obtaining a visa if your call requires one. Yet even opposition can indicate God's call. Some of the volunteers for our Summer Witnessing Campaign experienced such obstacles, and they served to strengthen the volunteers' determination to participate. When hearts are set on truly discerning God's call, opposition and temptations will not overshadow God's provision. He will provide the circumstances or experiences or whatever indications are necessary to confirm His call in your heart.

The Mystery of God's Call

Some people attach great mystical significance to the calling of God, the leading of God and the empowering by which God enables us to follow His leading. God does not play guessing games with His children—especially concerning those things He wants us to do. Nor is His calling a reward or sign of recognition of our virtue. Remember, God used Balaam's ass to convey His message. While the call of all believers is high, holy and heavenly, the mystery of God's call is that He is pleased to use weak and imperfect people such as you and me to His glory. If you want to be part of God's team to confound the wise, you have to be willing to become foolish. Whether we are called by God for a specific task or simply called to be His children, transformed into the likeness of Y'shua (and isn't that more than enough?), it is a mystery of grace that He chose to call us at all.

Y'shua said if the people who welcomed Him into Jerusalem were silenced, the stones would cry out in His honor. Some of us whom God is calling into ministry are just about as hardheaded! But hardheaded as we might be, let us also be humble. Why? 1 Corinthians 1:22-29 says it all:

> For Jews request a sign, and Greeks seek after wisdom; but we preach Christ crucified, to the Jews a stumbling block and to the Greeks foolishness, but to those who are called, both Jews and Greeks, Christ the power of God and the wisdom of God. Because the foolishness of God is wiser than men, and the weakness of God is stronger than men. For you see your calling, brethren, that not many wise according to the flesh, not many noble, are called. But God has chosen the foolish things of the world to put to shame the wise, and God has chosen the weak things of the world to put to shame the things which are mighty; and the base things of the world and the things which are despised God has chosen, and the things which are not, to bring to nothing the things that are, that no flesh should glory in His presence.

The High Road and the Low Road

The crowd moved down the road in a bright wash of sunlight. They had paid dearly to go on this journey. All had left the comforts of home; many had left family and friends who refused to make the journey themselves. But the fellow travelers soon became friends and family to one another, and as for home, they were headed for a new one—Gan Eden, the dwelling place of the Master.

The travelers reached a fork in the road. Someone pulled out a map and the group pressed in to see which path they should take. "Well," said the one with the map, "both paths lead in the right direction. See?" he said, pointing to a place on the map. "This one to the left is the low road. It'll take us down through a forest on a pretty level path. The high road to the right looks like a rocky desert climb. We'd be exposed to the sun with very little shade. I think the choice is obvious."

There was a murmur of assent and a general nodding of heads. But one young woman spoke up. "Wait," she said. "The master traveled the journey before us. I'd like to know which road He took. Is there some clue to help us find His path?" A few in the crowd nodded and looked expectantly to the man with the map. Most of the others had already begun to make their way down the low road, toward the forest. "Listen," said the map-holder impatiently, "both roads lead to the same place. Make things hard on yourself if you want to, but don't expect the rest of us to go along just because you want to prove how spiritual you are." He turned and followed the others.

The woman lowered her head. "I don't want to prove anything," she whispered to an unseen companion. "I just want to follow You." When she looked up, the crowd had disappeared. One elderly gentleman remained.

"The others took the low road, but it seems to me that you are right. Here's the clue you were looking for," he said, and pointed to a set of footprints on the dirt road to the right. Then he pointed out a single, continuous groove that began in the wake of the footprints and trailed after them as far as the eye could see. "The high road is the right one to be sure," he said, "because the one who went this way was carrying a cross."

The Weight of the Cross

Christians in general and many Jewish believers in particular don't talk much about the cross. Many of the mishpochah feel an aversion to it because it has often been a symbol of persecution for our Jewish people. We should not allow the wrongful acts attributed to the cross to obscure its true meaning. We need to clarify what the cross truly symbolizes so that our own hearts are rightly oriented.

Some people hang the cross on their dashboard, some wear it as a piece of jewelry. Most do not comprehend its weight, either in terms of the significance it holds, or the burden it imposes.

Y'shua didn't wear the cross, the cross wore Him! The purpose of the cross is not to provide decoration,[1] nor to provoke hatred and bigotry, though some misappropriate it for such purposes.

The cross as a symbol is a weighty reminder of the suffering, the separation and the pain Y'shua endured in order to reconcile us to the Father. It is an even weightier reminder that God has called us to endure some of that same suffering, separation and pain, because we are called to be and to do like Y'shua.

If we avoid the cross, we deny a call to suffer and to serve. There is no way to tailor or adjust the cross to make it comfortable. The cross is the instrument of service—the way by which Y'shua served God the Father, the way by which He served humanity. God chose the cross to convey His love to us, and it is the way by which we follow Him whether we find ourselves scrubbing floors or scrubbing up for surgery. The weight of the cross in terms of significance is its crucial role in enabling us to fulfill our destiny.

Don't expect many people to encourage you to take the high road of *cross-bearing*. You might find yourself lonely, and you might be surprised at how some respond if you ask them to come along. Otherwise friendly fellow travelers might say you are being proud, obstinate or insensitive to the feelings of others when you are simply trying to obey the Master. People, even

---

1. This is not to say that it is inappropriate to wear a cross, with or without a star of David. Some people choose to wear an outward sign of an inward commitment. But if the cross has no bearing on how a person lives his or her life, to wear it as an ornament is grievous.

other believers, who do not choose to bear the cross sometimes belittle those who do. That suffering, that burden of loneliness is part of the weight of the cross.

It is not natural or ordinary to want the cross, but overcoming our natural tendencies is part of the weight, the burden, of cross-bearing. It is natural to take "the path of least resistance," a path that provides personal convenience and comfort. Most of us would prefer that path, and I confess that I prefer it without a doubt. It is not the road to evildoing or gross sin. It is simply the low road, the ordinary path that allows us to say, "No need to push myself. I'll get there eventually."

The monotony of the low road lulls us into complacency, allows us to be content with the ordinary. The more accustomed we become to the low road, the more we begin to believe that we have a right to be and to do just like those around us.

Once we acclimate ourselves to the low road, there seems to be something distinctly undemocratic about that high road. The Declaration of Independence tells us, "We hold these truths to be self-evident, that all men are created equal, that they are endowed by their Creator with certain inalienable rights, that among these are Life, Liberty and the Pursuit of Happiness." The lure of the low road is its very ordinary assurance that travelers ought to have maximum comfort and minimal pain.

But how do "inalienable rights" hold up under the scrutiny of our Messiah's command to take up our cross and follow Him? How much happiness can we afford to pursue in view of the words of Y'shua: "He who finds his life will lose it, and he who loses his life for My sake will find it" (Matthew 10:39)?

"Truths" that ordinary citizens of this planet hold to be self-evident can become traps for those who are pursuing the way of Y'shua, the way of the cross. The weight of the cross is that He commanded us to take the way of service and self-sacrifice. We recognize the rights of others to pursue happiness. But what we recognize for ourselves is that we have extraordinary obligations that outweigh the rights others hold so dear. Do we have rights? Yes! We have the rights God gives to His own children—we are heirs with Y'shua. And that means we have inherited His cross and all it truly symbolizes.

The Way of the Cross

Every day, we face innumerable choices. Throughout our lives we make hundreds of thousands of decisions. Not all are the "high road/load road" variety, but we have more such choices than most realize. Too often we don't exercise choices; instead we allow habits to replace decisions or we just "let" things happen to us. But we can choose how to direct actions, words, tone of voice . . . even our thoughts. How often do we stop to wonder which path Y'shua would take?

Choosing the high road changes the way we relate to the world. Some believers take pride in the fact that their group or their way of doing things raises little or no opposition from the Jewish community. But what road must we take to find such acceptance? Could it be that the Jewish community doesn't object to that person or group because they haven't really understood the message? Could it be that the biblical "offense of the cross" doesn't come into play because the meaning of the cross and cross bearing was never expressed?

Our belief in Jesus is radical. It has always threatened the status quo and still does. Some people make concessions for the sake of giving the gospel a good image among unbelievers, forgetting that the image of Y'shua was to endure rejection from unbelievers. Regardless of methods, whoever clearly communicates that Jews as well as Gentiles need to trust Jesus as Messiah and sin-bearer will face opposition.

In taking the high road we show our commitment, not only by what we give, but also by what we give up. People naturally want to be affirmed, to be considered special. We need more people who are willing to be rejected by the world and are satisfied to be special to the Lord.

When Y'shua said, "If I be lifted up, I'll draw all men to me," He wasn't talking about being exalted. He wasn't talking about being feted. He wasn't talking about being celebrated. He was talking about being lifted up onto a cross.

It seems that God allows two ways for the believer, the high road and the low road. Yet He calls on His very best to make the commitment to the extraordinary path that few would choose. I admire those who have made the sacrifice to leave their homes and go overseas. For example, some of our mishpochah have chosen to live and serve in Russia, sometimes enduring harsh conditions for themselves and their families. These people have chosen the high road, the way of the cross.

For some people, taking the high road means giving up a lucrative career because God has called them to be evangelists. For others, it means staying in a secular career where they are passed over for promotions because they refuse to take the low road concerning certain business practices.

Children face decisions, just as adults do. Should they run away from the child who is said to have "cooties," or reach out to him or her and take the consequences? We cannot dictate these choices to children. We can only show them by example that we must sometimes make choices that do not put us in the best light as far as the world is concerned.

Each of us can recognize the "forks in the road" if we train ourselves to look for them. Here are some examples of choices we might face.

- Like any mishpochah, within the family of Jewish believers, we don't agree on everything. What if an unbeliever tells you that you are better than someone else in the mishpochah because you don't do such and such? How would you answer such an unbeliever?

- Imagine that you've just returned a day early from your vacation. Someone has left a "distress" message on your answering machine, hoping to speak to you as soon as possible. He or she doesn't expect you back in town for another day. When do you call such a person?

- A co-worker speaks to you in a way that he or she would never want to be spoken to. The "fork" in your road begins with what you *think* and continues with what you say. High road? Low road?

- Your unbelieving family has invited you to a reunion on the condition that you do not mention Y'shua, no matter which way the conversation might turn. What do you do?

The way of the cross always involves our willingness to

endure some degree of sacrifice or suffering. Some suffering comes as a result of our own sin and some comes as a natural occurrence in this life, but the way of the cross is a difficult road that we willingly choose. Y'shua was not the victim of a mob. He said plainly, "You have no power over me." Peter tells us, "For this is commendable, if because of conscience toward God one endures grief, suffering wrongfully. For what credit is it if, when you are beaten for your faults, you take it patiently? But when you do good and suffer, if you take it patiently, this is commendable before God. For to this you were called, because Christ also suffered for us, leaving us an example, that you should follow His steps" (1 Peter 2:19-21).

Choosing the high road will have an impact on the way we relate to the circumstances of life. Each of us needs to ask, "What have I given up? *What have I endured for the Lord that I did not have to endure?"*

The Wonder of the Cross

Forgive the mention of a rather silly movie, *The Santa Clause,* to illustrate an important point. I never saw the film, but I remember the television advertisements. In the story, an "average Joe" encounters Santa Claus, who, due to an accident, is unable to carry out his duties. He asks this average Joe to take his place, and when the guy dons the red suit, gradual changes begin taking place. His hair begins to turn white. He finds himself with a paunch around his middle. And of course, his beard grows at an amazing rate. Confused by these changes, he turns to a friend who shrugs and says, "Hey, you put on the suit, you become the big guy," or something like that.

Well, God did not send His son into the world to slide down chimneys, but Y'shua did come to bring the gift of eternal life—and that gift was made possible through the cross. There is something about taking up that cross that works a gradual, and yes, mystical transformation. We start to become more like Y'shua when we take on that cross, and that is why we need to take the high road. There is no sense in suffering for suffering's sake. There is no reason to take pride in persecution. But when we suffer because of our faith in Jesus, and when we accept rejection for

His sake, He uses our cross bearing miraculously to transform us.

Sharing the burden of the cross changes us in ways that no amount of studying, singing or even praying can. That doesn't mean that suffering for the Lord brings instantaneous spiritual maturity. But I would challenge you to consider whether any of us can hope to be like Jesus if we are not willing to take the path that leads to hardship and rejection.

There is a high road and a low road. The low road is to accept whatever comforts you can find along the way. The high road is to deny self and pick up your cross and follow Him. When you take the high road, you accept that anyone who doesn't understand Y'shua is not going to understand you. Anyone who hates the gospel will hate you. But that isn't all. When you love Y'shua, you love who He loves. And anyone who loves Y'shua will love you.

To follow in Y'shua's footsteps means that we not only share in his sufferings, but we also share in his victory. Miles J. Stanford wrote, "As our Substitute He went to the cross alone, without us, to pay the penalty of our sins; as our Representative, He took us with Him to the cross, and there in the sight of God, we all died together with Christ. We may be forgiven because He died in our stead; we may be delivered because we died with Him. God's way of deliverance for us, a race of hopeless incurables, is to put us away in the cross of His Son, and then to make a new beginning by recreating us in union with Him, the Risen, Living One."[2]

Our strength, that is the strength of the believer, is in allowing ourselves to be crucified. If we have died and our lives are in Messiah, what have we to fear?

Cross bearing is not joyless. Pain and anguish are mingled with the joy and satisfaction of fellowship with one another and fellowship with God. Someday, pain and anguish will be wiped away. Joy and satisfaction will burst into full bloom when the road to Calvary brings us face to face with the Crucified and Risen Lord.

---

2. Miles J. Stanford, *The Complete Green Letters;* (Grand Rapids, MI: Zondervan, 1983), p. 49.

The woman struggled on, much more slowly than when she began. No longer young, her feet and hands were callused and misshapened from years of grappling with the rocky terrain. Her face was worn and wrinkled by sun and wind. Her back was bent from the constant strain of climbing. Her traveling companion now leaned on her shoulder for support. As they made their way slowly over the next rise their eyes brightened. At last they beheld that for which they had been longing throughout the journey.

There before them lay Gan Eden. The mere sight of it was strength to their bones. Their pace quickened. No longer needing to lean on one another, their eyes shone to see the Master awaiting them at the entrance. He had come Himself to receive them! And as they stepped down off that high road into a luxurious carpet of thick velvety grass, they stood in silent awe because the place and person of the Master was so glorious and magnificent that words fail to describe it. Yet there were words spoken, words from the Master. His welcome transformed each scar from every wound suffered along the way into a radiant beam of light. The travelers found they had no more aches, nor pain, nor sorrow. They had only joy at their Master's greeting: "Well done, good and faithful servants."

Part Two
Walking With God's Family

Don't Give Up on Your Local Church!

"I enjoy the fellowship at church, but sometimes I feel out of place as the only Jew there . . . and sometimes I even feel a little guilty. I need encouragement and maybe some insights on how to deal with my situation," one Jewish believer confessed. And she is not unusual.

Ever feel like a hexagram peg trying to fit into a pentagram hole? Maybe no one else in your church thinks like you, talks like you, was raised like you and is rejected for their faith like you, simply because you are Jewish. You like the people in the church, but you seem to get lonely in a way that others don't. You feel like having the Lord in common should be enough, yet you miss having certain things in common: the memories, the humor, the heritage and odd bits of Jewish experience that only seem to make sense when you are speaking to another Jew.

It's not only the absence of other Jews that can make us feel like outsiders where we know we ought to belong. Most of us have on occasion encountered insensitivity to Jewish people in church. The fact that no harm is meant does not make it hurt less.

How many times have we overheard a fragment of conversation and caught a phrase like: "The price was too high, so I had to Jew him down," as if haggling over price was unique to Jews? While such remarks might not stem from outright anti-Semitism, they let us know we and our people are misunderstood. Then there is the well-meaning soul who cheerfully observes that you are not like other Jews—and means it as a compliment!

Other Jewish believers have the opposite problem—church members love their "uniqueness" and make them into overnight celebrities simply because they are Jews. The extra attention can be gratifying at first, but whereas unkind stereotypes are hurtful, overly positive ones embarrass us. The result is the same: we are reminded that we are different. When you know that you are different, yet you know you should fit in, feelings of alienation and ambivalence crop up.

The majority of our own Jewish people feel they must shut us out because of our faith. Naturally we wish to feel completely at home in the presence of those with whom we have common faith. But that is not always the case.

Sometimes we don't feel at home because of our own insensitivity and prejudices that can make everything in the church seem so strange, so *goyish*.[1]

Most of us feel uncomfortable with the symbols and trappings that many Christians appreciate. Few of us make use of golden crosses as jewelry, display pictures of Jesus or use ecclesiastical language. Some of our brothers and sisters find it difficult to separate what is cultural from what is truly spiritual. If we measured spirituality by their standards, we would feel it impossible to be ourselves. We chafe when certain forms of worship are presented as the model of "true" faith and practice because we know of other valid Christ-centered models. All these things can contribute to Jewish believers' feelings of ambivalence and alienation in a local church.

There are positive and negative ways to deal with the problem of ambivalence and alienation. One of the negative ways is to decide that it's not worth it. That seems to be the case with 26 percent of the Jewish believers whom Jews for Jesus surveyed in 1993. They simply avoid regular fellowship. Another response is to avoid or deny the significance of one's Jewish identity. A few attempt to assimilate or "blend" in with the dominant culture rather than grapple with being different. They refer to themselves as "former Jews."

Still other Jewish believers remain in their church but are not proactive on behalf of their Jewishness. Some even become "nattering nabobs of negativity," continually complaining about the church's defects and giving Jewish believers a bad reputation in the process.

But praise God, many Jewish believers in Jesus dig in, pitch in, take responsibility and accept their roles as part of the remnant in the church. They choose to overlook superficial defects that cause culture clash. They grow in faith and are usually a positive influence. They make a significant contribution to Jews and non-Jews within the body of Christ. They are a "credit" to the Jewish

---

1. *Goyish:* Gentile in character; alien to Jews.

people on the Christian "account." They make a commitment to "grow where they are planted."

The wisdom of "grow where you're planted" stems from the realization that leaving one fellowship makes it easier to leave another . . . and another. Such a pattern of leaving stunts growth and starves the soul. Don't risk spiritual starvation. Instead, help make your church a place where Christians of all walks of life can feel at home.

I do not oppose messianic congregations: places where Jewish believers can worship Y'shua in ways that are especially meaningful to us as Jews. However, I believe it is healthy for many Jewish believers to be members of evangelical churches. I base my view on the doctrine of the Universal Body, which we find throughout the New Covenant. The Apostle Paul expounds that doctrine beautifully in the following passage:

> For as the body is one and has many members, but all the members. . . are **one body** [emphasis supplied], so also *is* [the body of] Christ. For by one Spirit we were all baptized into one body—whether Jews or Greeks, whether slaves or free—and have all been made to drink into one Spirit. (1 Corinthians 12:12, 13)

Even so, it is difficult to dig in and say, "I am a part of this body," when non-Jewish culture and, in some cases, insensitivity to Jewish people can make us feel like outsiders. If you feel that way, you need to remember that being different from others in the body does not mean that you cease to belong in the body.

> If the foot should say, "Because I am not a hand, I am not of the body," is it therefore not part of the body? (1 Corinthians 12:15)

Diversity in the body of the Messiah can work to our advantage or disadvantage, depending on how we respond to those differences. *Often, our response is not so much how we feel about others, but how we feel about ourselves in relation to them.* If we are confident that we belong to Y'shua, it is much easier to appreciate the differences between ourselves and others.

The church possesses a wonderful dynamic of diversity and

unity. The two go together. Unity implies a way of dealing with diversity. **If we were all the same, we would have no unity; we'd merely have uniformity.** Unity amidst diversity demonstrates the ability to love and work together regardless of our differences. There is a certain fullness in unity that you don't have in uniformity. Compare singing in harmony to singing in unison. Both make good music. Both are good expressions of the Body of Christ. If the Body of Christ is a symphony of souls, then why shouldn't part of that symphony be played in unison and part in harmony?

Unity produces a testimony, and that is one reason we need Jewish believers in all kinds of evangelical churches. Unity leads to something else that we need individually and corporately:

> For the edifying of the body of Christ, till we all come to the unity of the faith and of the knowledge of the Son of God, to a perfect man, to a measure of the stature of the fullness of Christ; that we should no longer be children, tossed to and fro and carried about with every wind of doctrine. (Ephesians 4:12-14)

The word *perfect* is often translated as "mature," and in this context ("that we should no longer be children"), maturity seems a good choice. Unity and maturity go hand in hand.

Immaturity often manifests itself in the "self-exalting/other-deprecating" syndrome. There is a saying in Yiddish, *"Azde calle net tanzen zugse der klezmer kennet shpielen."* (When the bride can't dance, she says the orchestra can't play.)

Children learn to build up themselves and their friends by tearing down others. This practice often intensifies with preteens and carries through adolescence. "I could have made the team if I had tried. But who needs to join that bunch of losers?" Or, "What's so great about good grades? Good grades are for geeks who have nothing better to do than homework."

Putting others down is a sign of insecurity and immaturity. Any confidence gained by putting others down is false because it isn't based on any value within ourselves. One way to know when people are growing out of adolescence is to hear them demonstrate a well-placed sense of self-confidence. Mature people identify themselves according to their positive traits and abilities, as well as their affiliation with others whom they admire. Immature and insecure people rely on separation from others whom they portray in a negative way.

We recognize differences between ourselves and others, but those differences do not give us the right to create divisions. For example, I keep hearing a misnomer that causes me to cringe. It's the phrase, "Gentile church." For many, that is nothing more than an observation that the majority of people who claim to be Christians are not Jews. But I really think we have to stop using that term because it is just plain unbiblical. Regardless of the intent, the term allows creeping prejudices—and makes it difficult for many Jewish believers to be at home in the church of their choice. I don't think it is intended to be rude; nevertheless, I feel it's a divisive term.

Y'shua established *one* church. He told Simon Peter, "On this rock I will build My church" (Matthew 16:18). It wasn't simply a matter of adding a wing to an already existing structure. Y'shua is the Cornerstone that the builders rejected. Ordinary synagogues are not built on that chief Cornerstone. The church is. We can certainly continue using certain prayers and forms of worship that are in keeping with our Jewishness. But in substance, we are a new people. Jews don't become Gentiles and Gentiles don't become Jews—but we all become new creatures, new Jews and new Gentiles united in the Body of Messiah, which is the Church. The Church is a new organism that is neither Jewish nor Gentile, though it is made up of both.

When people speak of the "Gentile church," I don't think they really believe the Church underwent some form of mitosis, reorganizing itself into two separate entities. But those of us who worship in Messianic congregations need to be sensitive to the mishpochah who don't. How must they feel when they hear their community of worship described as the Gentile church? We are endangering our own mishpochah by making them feel they don't belong where the Bible says they do belong! We all belong with other believers in Y'shua, whether they are Jewish or Gentile, regardless of the cultures and forms of worship they practice.

Just imagine if *Gentiles* started referring to the "Gentile church." Picture them naming congregations "First Gentile Presbyterian Church," "St. John's Gentile Lutheran Church" or "Grace Gentile Baptist Church." We would be livid if they implied that Jews ought to be excluded! Yet, if we use the phrase "Gentile church," are we not implying that Jews don't belong? We can be thankful to God that the Church is not like that. Let's be careful not to foster the kind of separatist thinking that we would find hurtful if it were directed at us from others.

It is necessary and incumbent upon Jewish believers to have a positive attitude toward the Church and to the fullness of Gentiles that God desires to bring into His Church. In order to love our own children, we don't have to hate everybody else's. In order to encourage the growth of Messianic congregations we don't need to undermine mainline evangelical churches. And in order to encourage Jewish believers to maintain their Jewish identity, we don't need to transmit prejudices against Gentile Christian cultures and forms of worship.

There is no doubt that being the only Jew (or one of a few) in the local church can be uncomfortable. However, we want to be careful not to falsely impute motives of malice or bigotry. We are far more likely to encounter the ignorant remark or the insensitive joke from people who simply don't have the experience to know better.

How Can You Deal With the Problem of Insensitivity to the Jewish People Within Your Church?

It's important to remember that God wants us to tackle any problem we face by first bringing it to Him. We must remember that God not only has an opinion on these things, but He also has a will and He has a way of dealing with problems. He wants us to be part of His solution to what is essentially His problem.

As we draw closer to God, we become more secure in His love for us and more aware of His love for others. Then we can deal with those problems in a constructive, Christ-like way. So have a teachable spirit and ask God to help you deal redemptively with people.

That doesn't mean you should ignore offensive remarks. We

do not help an insensitive person by keeping silent, nor can we help other Jewish people who might come in contact with that person.

It isn't enough to say, "Please don't say or do _____ as it bothers me." You might get someone to alter behavior that way, but it won't help people to feel or sense what God wants them to feel. They might continue to think or say those things when you are not present.

People in the church need to know that it is not merely for your sake that you point out Jewish sensitivities. As believers, we have a spiritual patience and can choose not to take offense, but unbelievers will certainly take offense at insensitivity to or prejudice against Jews. Many of us Jews also were raised with stereotypes about Christians. One of those stereotypes says: "Scratch any *goy* [Gentile] and underneath you'll find an anti-Semite." We want to do everything possible to ease the underlying tensions.

Therefore, if something bothers you, *explain why in a way that shows you trust that the person who said it would care to understand.* We cannot help others feel with and for us if we demonstrate a lack of feeling for them in the process.

Avoid dumping a whole load of do's and don't's on non-Jewish Christians. You don't want them to feel they have to "walk on eggshells" any time they are around Jewish people.

As people respond with greater sensitivity over one issue, choose a time to remark on how much you appreciate their efforts. You might conclude such a remark with a statement such as, "I want to be sensitive to you as well. I hope you would let me know if there have been things I've said or done that didn't take your feelings into account." But you had better be ready to hear if there are!

Challenge stereotypes in a thoughtful way. If someone makes a remark about Jews and money, you might say, "That is a generalization that concerns me. Do you mind if I ask you a question? How many Jewish people have seriously discussed their value system with you?" The person might reply, "Oh, I didn't mean anything by that. I was just kidding." To which you might say, "I'm glad to hear that. But somebody who doesn't know you or have Christ in common with you is likely to take a comment like that at face value. I'd hate for anybody to believe you really think that way about Jewish people." Or you might take this approach, "Did you know that a number of my Jewish people live below the poverty level?" If their answer is no, you can go on to say, "I know that if you had a chance to meet more Jewish people you wouldn't have thought that."

Sometimes people hear a Jewish joke from a Jewish person and assume that we don't mind Jewish jokes. You might explain that Jewish humor tends to be self-deprecating in nature, but when it is enjoyed by others, it can seem cruel, because then we are not deprecating ourselves but being deprecated by others. It is appropriate to tell such a person (kindly) that many groups of people feel comfortable making jokes about themselves but do not enjoy hearing the same jokes from others. You can illustrate that point by mentioning siblings who call one another names at home but defend one another at school if anyone else uses the same names.

What if a person genuinely believes the stereotypes? Sometimes your own experience can be enough to set them straight, "You know, as I was growing up, money was always pretty tight in our family."

The main thing in dealing with the insensitivity of others is to decide what we want our own sensitivities to be. Sometimes we allow ourselves to take offense when we are faced with a matter of simple ignorance. We can and should help Gentile believers be more informed and sensitive regarding Jews. At the same time, we need to make sure that we are being more sensitive to what God tells us than we are to what other people say. When correcting others, we should do so in the same way and for the same reason that God corrects us. He loves us too much to let us be satisfied with ourselves in our present state of growth. Our desire to sensitize people in churches should come from that same love.

So please, don't give up on your local church, but take part in God's plan for reconciliation.

For He Himself is our peace, who has made both one, and

has broken down the middle wall of separation, having abolished in His flesh the enmity, that is, the law of commandments contained in ordinances, so as to create in Himself one new man from the two, thus making peace, and that He might reconcile them both to God in one body. (Ephesians 2:14-16)

Regardless of our background, regardless of our gifts, we all belong to Y'shua. In Him, we belong to one another. Let us rejoice! To feel at home with our Lord and Savior is the main thing. When we are immersed in Him, it's much easier to make ourselves at home with His people, in whatever setting. He brings us together.

Shepherds and Sheep

Once upon a time, not so many years ago, a fellowship of Jewish believers in Jesus had a vibrant and vital testimony for Y'shua. That fellowship was characterized by the strong leadership of one man and the supportive elders with whom he had surrounded himself. In fact, this man's influence extended beyond the small flock he pastored to several other Christian churches and institutions. In an area where there were few Jewish believers outside of this fellowship, many other believers admired the warm fellowship and sense of community that this messianic group enjoyed.

Then something went terribly wrong.

The leader began making "prophetic statements" that were declared authoritative for members of the fellowship. He proclaimed certain women in the group to be prophetesses. Gradually the voices of the "prophet" and "prophetesses" replaced the Word of God.

Eventually there was sexual misconduct between the leader and his special helpers. You can imagine how this tore the fellowship apart. Once the immorality was exposed, people questioned the entire structure and teaching of that fellowship, and rightly so. Much of it had not been kosher.

The congregation disbanded, but that wasn't the worst of it. When the "shepherd" fell (or when people realized he had fallen), the "flock" scattered. People were spiritually shell shocked. They did not know what to believe or whom to trust. Some former members renounced the Lord altogether. Others clung to their faith in Christ but refused to have anything to do with other Jewish believers.

Meanwhile many Christians who had extended their friendship and support to the fellowship were horrified by this—their only real contact with Jewish believers—and remain suspect of anything having to do with messianic Jews or Jewish evangelism *to this day.*

Obviously corruption and abuse of authority are not problems unique to Jewish believers. Sin is not the exclusive property of any people or sect, but when it rears its ugly head in a fellowship of believers—and particularly when it centers on the leadership—it brings disgrace to the whole community.

Those of us who are concerned with the well-being of the messianic flock need to take heed. Whether we are leaders or followers, the moment we imagine ourselves and our fellowship beyond danger is the moment we become vulnerable. Both shepherds and sheep need to recognize the kind of setup that can lead to a fall if we are to keep standing for Y'shua.

Remember that when we say "shepherd," unless we are talking about the Lord, we are actually talking about "under-shepherds." The psalmist wrote, "The Lord is my shepherd," and Y'shua clearly identified Himself as *the* Shepherd. God has appointed people to care for His flock, and we should be thankful for these under-shepherds. However not all who claim to be shepherds are good, God-appointed caretakers. In fact, sometimes wolves, rather than coming in sheep's clothing, prefer to dress up like shepherds.

We need to identify various kinds of wolves who would like nothing better than to scatter our little messianic flock, and then we need to be on the alert.

The Counterfeit Shepherd

He pretends to be your shepherd when he is not.

When we came to faith in Y'shua, we were born again. Whether Jew or Gentile, the only way to become part of God's flock is through Y'shua, the Good Shepherd. Anyone who does not truly represent Him cannot truly be our shepherd.

There are many leaders of the Jewish community who are not appointed by Y'shua. They are called rabbis, and they shepherd a different flock. For the most part they have little to do with us because they want to keep us away from "their" flock. Occasionally a rabbi takes an interest in members of the messianic flock, but not for the purpose of care and feeding. Their desire is to separate us from Y'shua. It is true that rabbis don't know Jesus is the Savior and the source of life, and they feel that to separate us from Him would be a good deed. But their intentions are beside the point so long as their purpose is to part us from our faith—a fact that has escaped many of the mishpochah.

Jews for Jesus sends out hundreds of surveys to Jewish believers every year. One question we ask is, "What do you feel is the greatest need for Jewish believers today?" Many respond, "Our greatest need is for the rabbis to accept us as Jews."

Do you remember Plato's parable of the cave? A community of cave dwellers sat together with their backs to the opening of their cave. All they knew of the outside world was from the shadows that were cast upon the wall of that cave. One man found his way to the outside world of sunshine and was amazed to see that what he had formerly known as dark shadows on the cave wall had substance, color and form beyond anything he could have imagined.

He returned to the cave but was unable to convey what he had seen to those who had never seen light or color. When he persisted in trying to describe the sun, the trees and the wonders of the world outside, his fellow cave dwellers regarded him as insane. Eventually someone decided that his eyes were the source of his pathology. So to cure the man, they put out his eyes.

We must never forget that as far as the rabbis are concerned, all Jewish believers in Jesus need to be cured. If they can't "cure" us, they want us isolated from the flock because what they regard as illness happens to be contagious.

Yet there are those in the messianic mishpochah who want to be accepted by rabbis, emulate rabbis or be flattered by the attention of rabbis.

Like sheep that people imagine jumping over a fence to raise slumber, some of our flock are jumping through hoops held by rabbis. Striving to prove their sincerity, their Jewishness or their ability to persuade, they continue prancing through those hoops until they have put themselves fast asleep, far from Y'shua's flock.

We need to realize that any rabbi who would be part of the flock of Y'shua must emerge from the new birth as a spiritual baby, just like the rest of us. To lead, they must have a mature walk with Y'shua. And unless they do experience the new birth in Christ, rabbis are the kind of shepherds we read about in Ezekiel 34. They are not shepherds we should be following.

The Hireling Shepherd

This false shepherd is after personal gain. Many such hirelings have been exposed by the media. Some had large television ministries and were not accountable to local congregations. Among the messianic mishpochah, hireling shepherds don't have quite as high a profile. They don't have large television ministries, but many do have several sources of income for which they are not accountable. They apparently are not paid enough by their congregation, so they set up organizations to receive donations from outside the congregation. Often when this happens, neither the congregation nor the organization is aware of how much the other pays that leader. That same leader might also seek financial gain for publishing books or pamphlets.

This does not mean that every shepherd who has more than one source of income is fleecing the flock. But they certainly are in a situation where greed might creep in unrecognized by themselves or their flocks.

Some shepherds do not start out as hirelings but end up that way because proper precautions are not taken. Congregations can and should help prevent this from happening to their shepherds.

Any shepherd who has more than one source of income *needs* to be accountable to his own congregation for whatever moneys he receives. A shepherd is not a salesman on commission or an entrepreneur; his income should not be determined by his own creativity or enterprising spirit. Congregations have elders and boards so that their leaders can receive the proper care as well as be properly accountable.

Some congregations are not meeting the needs of their leaders because they honestly can't. That's unfortunate. Some are not meeting the needs of their leaders because they have not made it a priority. Members might be living very comfortably, but it doesn't occur to them to sacrifice any of their comforts so that their pastor and his family can also live comfortably. That's even more unfortunate. The latter are sheep who are encouraging their shepherds to look elsewhere for support. They either don't realize or don't care that the shepherd has needs and that he has more important things to do than worry about how to meet those needs and the needs of his family. You don't want your shepherd to have to think too much about money. It prevents him from having a spiritual mindset.

That isn't to say that congregations are always to blame if they have a hireling shepherd. Some people take advantage of the fact that Christians can be overly trusting and "underly" discerning. Some people aren't satisfied with a comfortable living when they see the opportunity to grab more.

The New Testament describes the hireling shepherd as one who does not protect the sheep against wild animals that prey on the flock. That is because he puts himself first. If his own life or living is threatened, he finds somewhere else he needs to be—in a hurry. Such shepherds face the judgment of God. "Thus says the Lord God to the shepherds: 'Woe to the shepherds of Israel who feed themselves! Should not the shepherds feed the flocks?'" (Ezekiel 34:2).

The Devouring Shepherd

The third type of wolf in shepherd's clothing has doctrinal dentures. Rather than serving and tending sheep, he fleeces and devours them with false teachings. A whole spate of such shepherds seek to lead the mishpochah into heresy regarding the person of Y'shua and the nature of God.

Some deny the deity of Jesus; others deny the personhood of the Holy Spirit. Some say that Jews have a separate covenant with God and do not need the new covenant in Y'shua. Others dare to teach that everyone is saved through the new covenant whether or not they have faith in Y'shua.

There is no room for creativity when it comes to Bible doctrine and biblical theology. Yet people still heed these false shepherds because it is tempting to adopt comforting false beliefs—and difficult to stay true to sobering realities that spur us to action and make us vulnerable to rejection.

We have been warned in advance about devilish doctrines that false shepherds will feed all-too-willing sheep. "For the time will come when they will not endure sound doctrine, but according to their own desires, because they have itching ears, they will heap up for themselves teachers" (2 Timothy 4:3). These shepherds make it their business to go around scratching itchy ears, and in the process they stop up those ears so the truth won't get in. They will answer for every person they lead astray.

The Status-Seeking Shepherd

In Bible times, the youngest member of the family cared for the sheep. If an adult was given that task, it was not because he had a sterling résumé! When Jesus claimed to be the Good Shepherd, He gave dignity to what had always been a low status position. Dignity is a quality of quiet self-respect. It is not the same as pride. Yet today, some who claim to be shepherds are actually puffed up with pride over their position.

These shepherds may speak of glorifying Y'shua, but they are happy to receive adulation for themselves. They are actually addicted to the attention and soothing strokes they receive from the sheep. They need the flock more than the flock needs them, and sometimes they go to extremes to get or hang onto that flock.

This kind of false shepherd often builds on someone else's foundation. Sometimes he undermines another shepherd and presents himself as a "better" shepherd. His addiction drives him to collect as many sheep as possible without doing the work of evangelism to win them to the Lord. He isn't a sheep herder, he is a sheep stealer.

This type of status seeker might claim to have planted a congregation, but often he has not planted—he has "transplanted." He doesn't notice that such a transplant can loosen people from their spiritual roots. They might be weakened by transplant shock, or they might just decide that moving from one congregation to the next is acceptable at the first indication that their pastor or congregation is less than ideal.

Not all status-seeking shepherds are sheep stealers. Some are sheep smotherers. They are so possessive of "their" sheep that they view any other shepherd as a threat. They boost their status by insisting that members of their congregation come to them for "permission" to be involved with believers or spiritual pursuits outside their particular congregation.

People are often gratified and flattered by the close attention such leaders pay them. Yet for all the attention he gives, he does not help his flock to a place of spiritual maturity. If he did, they would see no scriptural basis for the tight reign he holds on them. He may spend much time with them in the Word, yet they remain unable to understand what the Bible really says without him to interpret it for them.

Status-seeking sheep stealers and sheep smotherers create problems because of their own needs. Very often these people have charisma and personal charm. Unfortunately, their need for status renders them ineffective as spiritual ministers. They have a fundamental misunderstanding of the work involved in being a shepherd.

Further, status-seeking shepherds often bolster their egos by claiming authority that God never gave. The Bible does say, "Obey those who rule over you [spiritual leaders] and be submissive" (Hebrews 13:17). But look at the context of that verse. The kind of spiritual leaders described are those who keep to sound doctrine, not giving strange or esoteric teachings. They are busy leaders whose lives set an example. They don't expect people to follow them because they possess special insights that are unavailable to others. They set a prime example in following that which was given to all of us. Their authority is not the authority of a parent over a child; it is the instruction they bring plainly from the Word of God.

When a status-seeking shepherd demands submission, those demands usually protect his own status rather than protecting the sheep. If members of the congregation begin serving the Lord apart from their minister's leading, this "shepherd" might even use his staff to beat them or his crook to hold that member back from a mature walk. After all, sheep who show too much dedication, too much spiritual concern for others, might reflect poorly on him.

Don't let a good shepherd go bad, and don't let a bad shepherd abuse the flock. Expect to hear sound scriptural basis for any requirements or restrictions that your pastor expects you to observe. When it comes to prophecy, remember that God does not reveal anything that contradicts what He has already told us in Scripture.

Having said that, if you feel that something is wrong with

your spiritual leader, prayerfully weigh your motivation. Be certain of your observations before raising an issue. Make sure that you do not become the kind of status seeker who enjoys being the center of attention at the expense of your pastor!

Some shepherds are false from the start. The very things that attract them to their positions make them likely to misuse authority. Other false shepherds start out as good leaders, but they fail to put on the whole armor of God, and they take a spiritual beating. Unfortunately, such spiritual beatings can easily go unnoticed.

When our resistance is down, sin finds a foothold in shepherds and sheep alike. We might become cynical about ministry, allowing standards to slip. Or we might believe ourselves somehow above those standards. We need to be the kind of flock that neither attracts false shepherds nor tolerates unsound leadership. When we have good leaders, we should appreciate them, because being the right kind of shepherd can be a thankless job.

No one ever called a ram the king of beasts. Sheep are not the most powerful, the fastest nor the most intelligent of animals. The fact is, sheep are not the most anything except maybe numerous. Yet God loves His sheep and wants them to be protected and nurtured. He takes a special interest in raising up shepherds who will take their job seriously and do it as unto the Lord.

Why else did God have Moses herding Jethro's sheep for so many years? It wasn't a punishment or a 40-year sentence that God imposed on Moses. It was His way of teaching patience, of gentling an easily angered, impatient man who was to lead our people to redemption. Moses' sheep herding experience helped him become a good shepherd for the flock of Israel. Rachel, whose name means "little lamb," tended her father's sheep—and became one of the great matriarchs of Israel. King David was a good shepherd as a boy, and he became the prototype of the Shepherd King who was to come.

When Y'shua described Himself as "the Good Shepherd," shepherding took on new dignity. All who shepherd the flock of God must recognize themselves as under-shepherds to the Great Shepherd, Y'shua. They must follow the pattern He set. To learn that pattern is the best safeguard against deception, not only for the shepherd, but also for the sheep. You've got to know what is authentic in order to spot a phony. John chapter 10 describes the Good Shepherd, and in that passage Y'shua describes four of His own qualities by which we recognize a good shepherd.

The Good Shepherd Knows His Sheep

It is mystifying how some people claim to be shepherds when they show no interest in the lives of the flock. One popular contemporary model allows pastors to stand in a pulpit and speak to huge audiences, behaving as though he is shepherding this massive flock when he is far removed from the everyday lives of those sheep. Such people are public speakers, not shepherds. They might have many worthwhile things to say, but they don't know the sheep.

Many people promote their own congregations by extolling the oratorical skills of their pastors. If a good pastor happens to be a wonderful speaker, that congregation is doubly blessed. But remember how the Apostle Paul described his shepherding ministry among the Corinthians: "I was with you in weakness, in fear, and in much trembling. And my speech and my preaching were not with persuasive words of human wisdom, but in demonstration of the Spirit and of power, that your faith should not be in the wisdom of men but in the power of God" (1 Corinthians 2:3-5).

My pastor demonstrates care and concern for me and for others in the congregation. He prays for us individually and takes seriously the admonition to care for the flock. Follow an under-shepherd who knows and cares for you.

The Good Shepherd Leads His Sheep

True under-shepherds demonstrate their credibility by their lives as well as their messages. Some under-shepherds act like cowboys riding high in the saddle, driving the flock across the plain like a herd of cattle. A good under-shepherd doesn't drive his sheep, he leads them—by example. His leadership is not based upon superiority; it is a function of trust and service for the purpose of enabling and equipping.

Good leadership helps a person grow to be and do more for

the Lord. It fosters a relationship with God whereby the person learns to make wise, Bible-based decisions without having to depend on the under-shepherd for each matter. Leading the sheep does not mean that the under-shepherd must always be in front. Sometimes he is beside the flock, coaxing and encouraging. Sometimes he is behind, gathering stragglers and protecting the flank. But he does not expect the flock to go because he is pushing. He does not lead them anywhere he has not been. And he doesn't spend his time and energy fighting with other shepherds. Follow an under-shepherd who leads by example.

The Good Shepherd Feeds His Sheep

Remember Y'shua's conversation with Peter after his resurrection? "Simon son of John, do you truly love me? . . . Feed my lambs" (John 21:15). Those under-shepherds who truly love the Lord show their love by doing all they can to provide food for the sheep. Notice that Jesus didn't tell Peter, "Feed your lambs," but "Feed *my* lambs." The sheep belong to the Lord, and the food must come from Him. That food is the Word of God, the Bible. The under-shepherd faithfully teaches, preaches and lives out the Word of God before the people.

In messianic circles we talk a lot about messianic lifestyles and Jewish traditions. These things matter to us, but under-shepherds are not called to concentrate on these issues. When it comes to lifestyles, all messianics should network to help one another with each other's Jewish identity in Jesus. The under-shepherd can help too, but we should not confuse help with working out one's Jewishness with feeding the flock. The main focus is not how to be Jewish, but how to be like the Jew, Jesus! Follow an under-shepherd who feeds you on the Word of God.

The Good Shepherd Gives His Life for the Sheep

Y'shua gave His life on the cross for all of us. Thankfully under-shepherds aren't usually called to that! But those who pastor God's flock should expect to make sacrifices for the well-being of the sheep. Ministry costs the minister something, and the price must be paid gladly, not grudgingly. Y'shua did not come to be served but to serve and give His life; even so the under-shepherd must have a servant's heart. Follow an under-shepherd who gives his life for the flock.

In addition to the many examples that Y'shua set for under-shepherds, one verse neatly sums up what a shepherd should and shouldn't be: "Shepherd the flock of God which is among you, serving as overseers, not by compulsion but willingly, not for dishonest gain but eagerly; nor as being lords over those entrusted to you, but being examples to the flock" (1 Peter 5:2-3).

If shepherds commit themselves to obeying this exhortation and if sheep expect their shepherds to hold to these standards, both shepherds and sheep will be led ever closer to the Good Shepherd, Y'shua.

These are standards for shepherds, but what about the flock? How should the true flock of God relate to a true shepherd?

1. *Regard him as an under-shepherd to the Good Shepherd who deserves your attention and respect.* The shepherd is supposed to know you by name, so don't regard his interest as an intrusion. That does not mean you are obligated to disclose every detail of your life, but when he wants to know how you are and how to pray for you, he needs a straightforward answer. On the other hand, do not monopolize your shepherd so that he is unable to tend to other sheep.

A word of encouragement is good, but much flattery is not. In fact, too much personal recognition makes a genuine under-shepherd uncomfortable.

2. *Support your minister.*

• Show enthusiasm for his ministry. When he preaches, sit close to the front and show that you are alert and eager to hear what he has to say.

• Give as generously as possible to support your own congregation. Inasmuch as possible, don't put the under-shepherd in a position of needing to look elsewhere to meet his needs and the needs of his family. A mature congregation wants to meet the needs of its own pastor, and to reach out to the unsaved as well. A young or struggling congregation does not need to be ashamed to receive help from outside but should view this as a temporary stopgap measure. The flock should not be satisfied if its pastor has to bring in other funds but should strive to meet his needs as well as the needs of the congregation. We don't want our movement to gain the reputation of *schnorrers!*[1]

- Pray for your minister. Pray for his spiritual and physical protection. If he is doing a good job, he is bound to be under attack. Remember to intercede for him, and enlist others to pray for him too!

- Speak well of the shepherd to others. Avoid gossiping or speaking ill of him. We're not supposed to gossip about anyone. Y'shua doesn't like it. When people gossip about a pastor, they undermine that pastor's ability to serve. Of course, if there is a serious problem of moral turpitude, deal with it in a scriptural way. But don't pick at nits. Remember, your pastor is an under-shepherd with human weaknesses and faults just like the rest of us.

3. *Stick with one shepherd rather than grazing with several different flocks.* That doesn't mean you shouldn't discuss spiritual issues with others. It means that you shouldn't hop from one congregation to the next. A sheep who roams from one congregation to the next can easily become a maverick due to the lack of accountability. Such sheep put the under-shepherd of each flock they visit in an awkward position of wondering, "How do I minister to this person?"

Furthermore, pastors do not feed sheep for the sake of getting them fat. Sheep are supposed to receive ministry and grow in the Lord so that they can minister to others in return. Sheep who roam from one congregation to the next only to sample what they can get are in no position to give because they do not involve themselves in the life of any congregation. Not only is a congregation deprived of their gifts, but they are depriving themselves of the satisfaction of truly belonging.

---

1. *Schnorrers:* unscrupulous beggars; those who are always seeking a handout.

4. *Take on some responsibility within your congregation.* Don't expect the pastor and one or two "pillars of the congregation" to do everything and arrange everything. Instead of regarding a congregation as "his" [your minister's] congregation, think of it as "our" congregation. Instead of complaining that this or that isn't good, invest yourself in making it better. The needs of a congregation are many, so there are numerous commitments one can make: helping with the children's program, ushering, serving on a committee to help decide the direction of the congregation's ministry, helping with refreshments, helping to keep the facility clean, bringing meals to members who are ill—and those are just starters.

God has promised that one day we will all be directly under the care of our Messiah. "I will establish one shepherd over them, and he shall feed them—My servant David. He shall feed them and be their shepherd" (Ezekiel 34:23). We can all look forward to that day. And for those who are faithful in fulfilling their duties as under-shepherd, "when the Chief Shepherd appears, you will receive the crown of glory that does not fade away" (1 Peter 5:4).

In the meantime, we need to help one another be the kind of shepherds and sheep that bring glory to God. So, "May the God of peace, who brought up our Lord Jesus from the dead, that great Shepherd of the sheep, through the blood of the everlasting covenant, make you complete in every good work to do His will, working in you what is well pleasing in His sight, through Y'shua HaMashiach, to whom be glory forever and ever. Amen" (Hebrews 13:20-21).

What About Jews for Jesus and Messianic Congregations?

Jewish believers in Jesus don't agree on everything, nor do we need to as long as we agree on who Y'shua is and what He means to us. Nevertheless, disagreements are not ideal, and we should definitely do away with those that are not based on reality, especially if they cause division. For example, people tell me that Jews for Jesus is against Messianic congregations, that is, congregations of Jewish and Gentile believers who love Jesus and worship in a Jewish format. Some regard this as a proper stand, while some who are involved with Messianic congregations are understandably disappointed. **Frankly, both reactions disturb me because Jews for Jesus is not against Messianic congregations.**

It is difficult to pinpoint why some people attribute this position to us, with the exception of one lady who said she actually heard our founder, Moishe Rosen, talk about Messianic congregations. She was referring to an informal question and answer session at a Jews for Jesus Ingathering. I recall such a session in which Moishe expressed concern and criticism of specific tendencies or patterns that he sees as dangerous to the movement, but that did not constitute an adversarial position toward all Messianic congregations. In an informal setting, it would not be difficult to prompt Moishe to express concerns and criticisms of any number of things he cares about—including the Jews for Jesus staff!

Whoever said that love is blind? The more important something is to us, the higher we set our hopes and expectations. Support does not call for unconditional affirmation, and criticism does not indicate blanket disapproval. God calls us to a higher kind of commitment to one another.

If you know anything about Jews for Jesus, you know that our passion and primary commitment is the evangelization of our Jewish people. Perhaps we have not said enough to make people aware of some of our other commitments, including those regarding Messianic congregations. I'd like to make known a few simple facts.

- When Jews for Jesus founder, Moishe Rosen, began his ministry under the American Board of Missions to the Jews (now Chosen People Ministries) in the 1950s, he regularly preached at a Friday night congregation in Brooklyn.

- He also conducted services at Congregation Beth Sar Shalom, first in Hollywood and then in New York City, back in the 1960s when Messianic congregations were few and were not called Messianic congregations.

- Many people on the staff of Jews for Jesus, myself included, are members of Messianic congregations.

- We often refer new Jewish believers to Messianic congregations in their areas, and we often ask Messianic congregations to help follow up on contacts who respond to our evangelistic campaigns.

If you had any question about Jews for Jesus and Messianic congregations, I hope that the above information has helped to clarify our support.

Nevertheless, there are some who want to draw a line dividing Jewish believers from one another based on false characterizations. These individuals have done us all a disservice by creating unnecessary division between us.

So we don't always agree. Natural brothers and sisters don't always agree! They are still family and they still need one another. Likewise, there aren't enough of us to divide or separate ourselves from one another. Yet it isn't on the basis of mere numbers that we need to be careful about divisions. Let's agree to disagree and thus avoid the mistake the Bible warns us about: "For where there are envy, strife, and divisions among you, are you not carnal and behaving like mere men? For when one says, 'I am of Paul,' and another 'I am of Apollos,' are you not carnal?" (1 Corinthians 3:3-4).

I hope this chapter has dispelled the notion that Jews for Jesus is against Messianic congregations. I'd like to go a step further and explain my personal support of Messianic congregations.

The congregation my family attends is called Tiferet Israel, and we worship on Friday evenings. I love my congregation and for several years I took an active part in planning services. We have a well-developed Messianic liturgy including the Amidah,[1] the Aleinu,[2] the Sh'ma[3] and liturgy for the Torah[4] service. Several of us worked to develop new aspects of liturgy to strengthen the worship at Tiferet Israel. We want our services to be Y'shua centered, and we want to strengthen the Jewishness of our worship in the process.

I appreciate the opportunity to express my Jewish identity in corporate worship. That is one of the real advantages of Messianic congregations. I don't think all Jewish believers need or ought to be members of Messianic congregations, but for me, it is an opportunity to commit time and energy to a local fellowship of believers and meet a personal commitment to maintain my Jewish identity at the same time.

Another reason I am a member of a Messianic congregation is that my children benefit from it. They learn about Y'shua through Jewish eyes, they relate to other children of Jewish believers, and they already know many of the prayers, which I feel enrich our corporate worship as Jewish believers. I think we could do much more to develop a children's program at my congregation, and if there is one area in which I would like to invest more of my time, it would be that one.

As the son of Messianic Jewish parents, I know the struggles of fostering a child's Jewish identity within the context of a predominantly Gentile congregation. Most of the second generation children who maintain their identity as Jews have done so because their parents were involved in some outside organization, whether it was a Jewish mission or a group such as

---

1. *Amidah:* a portion of the worship service when the congregation stands as a sign of respect and devotion; in the synagogue it refers to 18 specific benedictions (the *Shemoneh Esray*) in the siddur (Jewish prayer book) that are recited while standing.

2. *Aleinu:* a prayer of praise to God, used to end Jewish worship services— it begins with the Hebrew word *aleinu* (literally upon us, meaning it is our obligation).

3. *Sh'ma:* the most important prayer of Judaism that begins, "Hear, O, Israel . . ."; in the synagogue it encompasses Deuteronomy 6:4-9, 11:13-21 and Numbers 15:37-41.

4. *Torah:* the Law as contained in the Pentateuch; the five books of Moses.

the Hebrew Christian Alliance (now called the Messianic Jewish Alliance of America). Now I can count on my children having their Jewish identity reinforced, not only in our home, but also at our congregation.

I also appreciate Messianic congregations because they beautifully illustrate the collapse of the middle wall of partition. The breaking of that barrier is vital to the Body of Messiah. As messianic leader Dan Juster points out,

> Although Messianic Jews have a distinct calling from God, they are part of the Body of Messiah universal! . . . Although we seek to be part of Israel, we are also one with the Body of Messiah Jesus. Our words should reflect this. Our deeds should reflect this as well. There should be joint services, cooperative fellowship with leaders, etc. We can learn from the whole Body as we hopefully enrich it as well.[5]

My wife Patti, who is not Jewish, has been received as an equal member at my congregation, and that is important to me. I'll be the first to say that we must maintain the Jewishness of our Messianic congregations. It would be most difficult for a Messianic congregation to reinforce the Jewish identity of its members if the majority of those who attend were not Jewish. Nevertheless, we cannot raise up a middle wall of partition or make Gentiles feel like second-class citizens in a Messianic congregation. This is a fine balance that, at times, can be difficult to keep.

When Gentile spouses or singles seek to affiliate with our congregation, the pastor usually meets with them and clearly explains our vision. We have both a general and specific purpose statement in our bylaws:

> General Purpose: The general purpose of this Congregation shall be to preach the Gospel, to administer the ordinances of Y'shua, to minister to the spiritual needs of its members and all people everywhere, to train believers

---

5. Daniel Juster, *Jewish Roots: A Foundation of Biblical Theology for Messianic Judaism* (Pacific Palisades: Davar, 1986), p. 249.

to work for the Lord, and to further the evangelization of the world by bringing the Word to men, women and children so that they may enter into a living faith in Y'shua HaMashiach (Jesus Christ). Specific Purpose: The specific purpose of this Congregation is to win Jewish people to the Lord Y'shua, to help them build their identity in Y'shua, and to affirm their Jewish cultural identity.[6]

Gentile Christians who understand, affirm and agree to help us carry out both those purposes are welcomed at Tiferet Israel. I think this stipulation, along with the fact that our service has a fair amount of Hebrew liturgy, has helped us to maintain the Jewish identity of our congregation and its members.

I love the fellowship of the Body of Messiah, and I love to be with brothers and sisters of various cultures and backgrounds. Yet I especially appreciate the fellowship of other Jewish believers in Jesus, and I know that when I go to my congregation, I will find that fellowship. It is not necessarily wrong to gravitate toward those who share similar cultural background. When Asian-Americans or African-Americans worship in churches that express their culture and background, they are not required to justify their preference, nor should they be. Why should it be different for Jewish believers?

Whether we are Jewish or Gentile, male or female, makes no difference when it comes to our standing before God. But those differences are not obscured in every area of life. Even in the New Testament there existed the Jerusalem church, which was predominantly Jewish, and the Roman church, which was predominantly Gentile.

Most evangelical churches in America today are peopled with members who have common cultural roots. Today's Messianic congregations are a natural outgrowth of what missiologist Donald McGavran has called a "people movement."[7] When a significant number of people from a particular group come to

---

6. Bylaws of Congregation Tiferet Israel, a California Nonprofit Religious Corporation (1993).

7. Donald A. McGavran, *Understanding Church Growth* (Grand Rapids, MI: Eerdmans, 1970), p. 334.

Christ, they are more likely (when possible) to remain together in indigenous fellowships rather than expressing their faith within the context of someone else's culture.

What we don't want to do is so closely identify with our own people group and culture that we alienate the rest of the Body of Messiah. We would lose much if we were to cut ourselves off from our non-Jewish brothers and sisters. One thing that I appreciate about Tiferet Israel is that we have affiliated with the Baptist General Conference (BGC). We are an independent and self-supporting congregation, not dependent upon the denomination or any other organization for our continued existence. Nevertheless, we have this connection, this fellowship, with a world-wide body of believers that reflects the universality of our faith. I see this as another demonstration of the breaking down of the middle wall of partition.

Not only is our congregation self-supporting (we don't solicit any funds from outside people or organizations), but we also support agencies outside our congregation. Our budget includes regular donations to Jewish missions as well as a local rescue mission in San Francisco, our local Crisis Pregnancy Center and Inter-Varsity Christian Fellowship. In addition, many members give to world-wide missions via the "unreached peoples" program of the BGC. Ours is not a large or particularly wealthy congregation, but thus far God has enabled us to reach out, and I know of other congregations that have a similar vision.

Ours is not the only Messianic congregation to affiliate with the BGC, and many congregations have affiliated with other established organizations such as the Assemblies of God and the Southern Baptist Convention. We also have the Union of Messianic Jewish Congregations (UMJC), the International Association of Messianic Congregations and Synagogues (IAMCS) and the Fellowship of Messianic Congregations (FMC). Such groups facilitate cooperation and accountability and serve to strengthen Messianic congregations.

Finally, I appreciate the way that Messianic congregations provide a testimony to the Jewish community concerning Y'shua and the good news of the gospel.

I'm glad to be able to tell Jewish neighbors that we worship in a Messianic congregation. When an unbelieving Jewish person shows interest in the Messiah, I can bring them to a congregation that is recognizably Jewish. However, I do not go to a Messianic congregation just so that I can tell Jewish neighbors that I do, nor is Tiferet Israel's liturgy for the benefit of unsaved visitors. Nor do I agree with those who say that Jewish believers belong only in a Messianic congregation.

We Jews for Jesus do not believe there is one kind of congregation where we should worship or that there is one "style" of service for Jewish believers. When it comes to worship at home or in the congregation, we think it is a matter of the heart and the conscience.

I know some people have said that Messianic congregations are "the most effective means of spreading the kingdom." Yet a survey done by Michael Schiffman, leader of Congregation Kehilat Y'shua in New York, showed that only 2 percent of the Jewish believers surveyed came to faith in Messiah through Messianic congregations.

That in no way detracts from the value of Messianic congregations! Nor does it mean that Messianic congregations should not strive to build their testimonies and outreach programs. It *does* mean that the primary value (not the only value, but the primary value) of congregations is ecclesiological, not missiological. We would do well to remember and communicate that. If it were not so, most of us involved in Jewish missions would gladly choose an easier, more popular vocation. We would rejoice if more seeds could be planted and more Jewish people could be won through congregations than through mission outreach, but that notion is unsubstantiated.

Well-known missiologist Ralph Winters points out the New Testament pattern by which congregations and missionaries worked together to bring about a proclamation of the gospel. He uses the words *modality* and *sodality*. The modality was the local congregation whether it be the Jerusalem or Antioch congregation. The sodality was the apostolic band such as Paul and Silas: those who went out from the congregation to carry on the work of ministry. The work of the apostolic band strengthened the congregation and resulted in new congregations.

The congregation was the *fruit* of proclamation not the *method* of proclamation.

This model functions in the same way today. Organizations such as Jews for Jesus are single-issue sodalities, and Messianic congregations are modalities. We work hand-in-hand for the furtherance of the kingdom. Like the apostolate, the sodalities, or missions, exist for the purpose of proclaiming the message of the gospel to our Jewish people. Messianic congregations are modalities that exist as an expression of the universal Body of Messiah in a particularly Jewish cultural context. There will naturally be a distinction between the missions and the congregations, but if we do our jobs well, the work that missions do ought to add to the Messianic congregations, and some of the best missionaries might also be sent out from the Messianic congregations. We ought, therefore, to be supportive of one another.

A number of years ago it was popular to wear a button that read "PBPGIFWMY." The letters stand for "Please be patient, God isn't finished with me yet." All of us in the Messianic move-ment could be wearing those buttons. We all need to be more humble and extend more grace to one another. If we really want the revival we talk about and pray for, then we will emphasize the things that unite us. Jewish believers who are members of tradi-tional evangelical churches should support and encourage those in Messianic congregations and vice versa. Jewish missions should be supportive and encourage Messianic congregations and vice versa.

I won't say that we should pretend each one is perfect, since none of us is! I hope we are all growing in our ability to both give and receive constructive criticism. Unfortunately, within the mishpochah we sometimes disagree on what is constructive! Such disagreements, however, should not define our relationships or cause us to distance ourselves from one another.

The Bible says, "Test all things; hold fast what is good" (1 Thessalonians 5:21). I want to hold fast to what I know is good, and I want you, dear mishpochah, to know that as far as I'm concerned, there is much that is good about Messianic congregations.

Distinct or Divided?

The table was laden with a sumptuous feast. No one would be hungry after this repast! Better yet was the satisfying fellowship: the lively conversation, the laughter and the warmth that each person felt being together with friends "cut from the same cloth." But all that changed in a moment with a knock at the door.

It was as if a cold wind swept into the room along with those who entered. An entertaining story seemed to die on the lips of one who just seconds before seemed so animated, so enthusiastic. The story would seem silly to the newcomers, he reasoned.

Some who were seated at the table suddenly found their meal distasteful. Plates were quickly pushed away as though the food on them was an embarrassment. Newcomers were shown to their own table. A few from the first table, who could no longer enjoy what had been a warm lighthearted celebration, joined them.

Those left sitting at the first table couldn't hide their disappointment. They continued to eat, but the food had lost its savor, along with the lively conversation that quickly dwindled to a few mumbled sentences. The genial fellowship became a dull, frigid gathering of two groups sitting at separate tables.[1]

We need to ask: what binds people together? What pulls them apart?

Language, culture and neighborhood are common denominators that simultaneously bind together and separate individuals and groups.

Social scientists consider religion one of the most potent forces to unite and divide people. Many blame religion for division and its often violent and destructive consequences.

History records episodes of religious people who banded together and turned against others of differing religions—or even against others who adhered to the same basic religion but were of a different branch or denomination. Yet what we call "religion" has

---

1. This illustration is just my idea of what the situation that Paul described in Galatians 2:11ff might have been like. It is not meant to be in any way representative of any particular groups or individuals today.

no mind of its own; it doesn't act of its own accord. It cannot unify or divide; it is only animated by people who profess the religion.

God is not religion and can't be contained by any religion. He has recorded His own account of His important dealings with humanity. In the record of God's sacred history, true faith in Him is an active force to unite people.

Most of the Scriptures tell of God's dealings with the Jewish people. It is important to remember that God called Israel to be separate from the other nations. Our clothing was to be different, our food was to be different, even our celebrations were to be different. Circumcision was irrevocable. Even if we dressed in the clothing of our enemies, when standing naked we would be seen to be Jews. We were not only separated by circumcision, rituals, dress, etc., but we were also separated into a land, and we were separated by a law.

It is also good to remember the purpose of that separation. It was to keep God's people from idolatry and the evil practices of their heathen neighbors. This separation was to glorify God and accomplish His purposes. The climax of God's great purpose and promise to Abraham was that "in you all the families of the earth shall be blessed" (Genesis 12:3). He spoke through Isaiah to say:

> It is too small a thing that You should be My Servant to raise up the tribes of Jacob, and to restore the preserved ones of Israel; I will also give You as a light to the Gentiles, that You should be My salvation to the ends of the earth. (Isaiah 49:6)

When God separated the Jews as a people, His ultimate intention was to restore, reunite and heal. He separated the Jews because He wanted to benefit all.

It seems that some of our Jewish people mistook God's calling. For some, Israel's particularism became an end rather than a means to fulfill God's purpose. Some of our people thought we Jews were to remain separate because we were somehow better in and of ourselves. To illustrate, some Jewish people have no particular belief in God yet would be mortified if their children married "outside." Yet if there is no God and if the Jewish religion is myth, why should it matter?

For others, the whole idea of blessing and salvation has been downgraded from the transcendent to the ordinary realm of human abilities and the many worthwhile yet secular contributions we have made to society. Such people might have a vague idea that God has somehow blessed Jews with more creativity, more intellect, and that we owe it to God and to the human race to use these gifts to make the world a better place.

Either way, God's purpose of universal blessing has been sacrificed on the altar of our inadequate interpretation of chosenness. Yet our mistakes do not thwart God's plans. Israel's greater Son, Y'shua, became the Servant through whom God would pour out His blessing on this divided and divisive world. Thus far only a minority of Jewish people have received the blessing that comes through knowing Jesus, but millions of people representing thousands of nations have indeed been blessed by knowing Him.

When Messiah died on the cross and rose again from the dead, He not only smashed the barrier of sin that separated all of humanity from our Creator, He also tore down the wall of division between peoples, establishing a profound and eternal bond between individuals of diverse backgrounds.

It seemed good to God, the Holy Spirit and the Jewish disciples gathering at Jerusalem to welcome non-Jews into the place of grace (Acts 15). The spiritual bond was stronger than any racial, national or ethnic connection. This is the triumph of the Servant of the Lord. He turned our failure into victory. Hallelujah!

Truly God is gathering a people for Himself from every kindred tribe and nation. The wonderful, beautiful, delightful thing is that He didn't ask all the other people to give up their cultures and become Jews, and today, although there are fewer Jewish believers than Gentiles, we are not called to give up our Jewishness either. No culture is to be exalted over another; Jews and Gentiles can remain distinct yet our distinctiveness should not serve to divide us.

Those in Christ represent countless cultures, each with their own heritage. It is important to distinguish between diversity and division. As Jewish believers, we do not need to be protected or separated from Gentile Christians, for these who are true followers of Y'shua will not tempt us into idolatry or other immoral practices.

Instead of separating us from non-Jews, God has woven us together with Gentile believers into one seamless, rich and colorful fabric of love and unity. This is the beauty of diversity. However, much has happened to pull at that multicolored, multitextured fabric.

A Different, Perhaps Better, Era

Whenever revival comes, it unites us and strengthens our togetherness in the Lord. Some of you who have walked with the Lord for more than 20 years remember the joy of knowing Jesus toward the end of the sixties and into the first few years of the seventies. Any believer in Jesus who recognized another had a ready word of encouragement. We waved to one another as we saw the testimony bumper stickers or T-shirts, whether or not we would choose their particular slogan for ourselves. There was new music, a new sense of earnestness and a generally "up" feeling during the Jesus Revolution.

It was especially great to be a Jew who believed in Jesus during those years. So many of us who had been lonely suddenly discovered that there were actually hundreds, even thousands of Jewish brothers and sisters who loved Y'shua just like we did.

But soon enough, people began marking out their own "territory." That seemed to signal the end of that particular outpouring of the Holy Spirit. The sweet unity, mutual encouragement and acceptance dwindled, and for some it gradually ceased. People began to identify themselves with other people instead of being content to say they were "Jesus people."

Then there was an offishness of some Jewish believers toward one another. What started as lines drawn on the ground became small fences. And the small fences grew into larger walls. And the walls have continued to grow to the point where they are ominous and foreboding.

It's sad when Jewish believers who really need each other choose to distance themselves from one another. Or worse yet, they accept the divisions and distinctions made by those who are not believers! Many staff and friends of Jews for Jesus have been hurt and dismayed by statements such as this one published in the *Jerusalem Report:*

> Jews for Jesus and groups such as Chosen People Ministries and Ariel Ministries . . . are primarily devoted to coaxing Jews into joining evangelical Christian congregations. Messianic Jews, while they also proselytize, are more concerned with developing their own community of people who profess to follow both Jesus and traditional Judaism—a leap of faith that requires no formal conversion.

Jews for Jesus are accustomed to negative statements and false characterizations from the Jewish press, which feels obligated to oppose us. But it seemed there might be a different tactic at work here. Could it be that this drawing of distinctions between Jewish believers was designed to "divide and conquer"? If so, then it seems that our opposition may have found a few unwitting allies among our own believing mishpochah. We are now hearing some of our fellow Jewish believers saying strange things—implying that we don't really care to be Jewish, that we simply want to "feed" Jewish believers into churches, as though churches are somehow waiting to chew them up and spit them out without a shred of Jewishness remaining!

I know there are leaders in the unbelieving Jewish community who are absolutely convinced of our Jewishness, though they continue to declare that we are not Jews. They can justify the fact that they know one thing and say another because they believe they are protecting the flock. But when our own mishpochah begin to repeat what the opposition says, who are they protecting, and from what?

Maybe you have seen the commercial for a particular car rental agency. The ad features some poor family that failed to choose the "right" rental agency. We see them in a broken-down auto they foolishly rented from the other guy. It's dark. They are on some deserted stretch of highway, stranded, their vacation ruined. If only they had chosen the right agency, they would be cruising down a sun-drenched coastal road enjoying the most gorgeous scenery imaginable. We all understand the ploy. We smile. We don't take it seriously, but maybe we will rent from the "right" agency anyway.

There is a different kind of advertising, the kind that focuses on what makes a product unique and valuable without reference to competitors. So confident are the advertisers in the quality of their products that they have no need to cast aspersions on anyone else.

It is fine for various Jewish missions or Messianic congregations to express their distinctiveness. But can't we do so without making negative insinuations or implications about the commitments and distinctiveness of others? We can if we are confident of our own identity and careful not to be drawn into someone else's agenda. None of us should presume to be a spokesperson for another except in those matters where we *know* that we are in agreement!

It takes some commitment and planning for us to do right by one another. If someone asks, "Well, how are you different from so-and-so?" how would you respond? I would not consider that an appropriate question, and I hope that some of you will reconsider whether it is appropriate for you to answer it as well.

At Jews for Jesus we are aware that because our name is a statement as well as the name of an organization, many people mistakenly think that all Jewish believers are either on our staff or agree with everything we say and do. We sympathize with the need for other organizations to have their own identities, and we understand that there are legitimate differences of opinion whereby some are uncomfortable being thought of as part of our organization.

Actually, it is a door that swings both ways. There are certain policies held by members of our mishpochah that we disagree with and would not want ascribed to us. But we will not dissociate from those with whom we disagree, and we will not attempt to describe to outsiders why certain members of the mishpochah do or say things with which we differ. The differences cannot possibly be more important than the sense of unity and respect for one another that Y'shua wants us to have.

When we (meaning any Jewish believer) assert our own identity, whether as a spokesperson for a congregation, a mission, an umbrella organization or an individual, we should speak for ourselves or for those who have asked us to speak for them. We should not speak for others. That means not engaging in a discussion of how we are different from anyone else in the mishpochah. To assert your identity, you need only speak for yourself. Let others speak for themselves.

What can we do when someone asks, "How are you different from so-and-so?" Why not answer, "I really appreciate your interest in my mission/congregation/organization/self. Here is what we are all about. . . . As for how we differ from so-and-so, I think I'm more qualified to tell you how we are the same. I know that so-and-so also believes that Jesus (or Y'shua/Yeshua) is the Messiah predicted by the Jewish prophets. I know they believe that Jews as well as Gentiles need to find reconciliation through Him. As to how we are different, I think so-and-so is better qualified to state their distinctiveness than I. Why don't you ask them about their mission/congregation/organization/self and you can decide for yourself how we are the same and how we are different.

What if the person says, "But I understand you used to be a member of _____ congregation," or "Weren't you on the staff of _____? I thought you would be knowledgeable about them."

Most people can be tempted to show that they are knowledgeable under such circumstances. But stop and think. Would that congregation, would that mission, would that organization consider your past affiliation with them a good basis for you to represent them today? Or to represent them in those areas where you differ in opinion?

We owe it to Y'shua to treat one another with respect and fairness, and that means not taking the liberty to be a spokesperson for someone with whom we feel we have a difference. This is especially true when there has been a congregational split or when people break an affiliation due to disappointment that one or the other (or both) feel. Perhaps we believe we have not been treated fairly in such a situation. All the more reason not to do unto others what we did not appreciate having done unto us!

God ordained a unity that we dare not ignore. Each Jewish person who believes in Y'shua is part of the "remnant according to the election of grace" (Romans 11:5). Unity does not mean that we will always agree with one another. It does mean that areas of disagreement do not give us the right to condemn or shrink away from one another. Such behavior often sets off a chain reaction that becomes a "vicious cycle."

When people feel they have been rejected, they are hurt. Sometimes they deal with that hurt by rejecting those whom they feel have judged or rejected them. Unfortunately, and to the shame of the mishpochah, the cycle can get pretty vicious. It's no comfort to know that this is the case, not just with Jewish believers, but in the Body of Messiah in general. It's just a very human failing.

I need to avoid that trap and so do you. Y'shua is probably the only one in history who hasn't fallen into this trap at some time. It's the moment in which we feel stung by something someone has said that we are most likely to fall.

Sometimes we do sting one another with criticisms, perhaps in the hope of alerting one another to problems that ought to be addressed. Other times, the sting stems from a less noble source, such as hurt feelings over a "she said that he said . . . " interaction. Many people feel important or wise when they fault others, so they complain about or denigrate brothers and sisters.

Whether or not we expect our comments to be repeated, we need to realize and take responsibility for the fact that when we put others down, we risk alienation for a moment's gratification. We need to be careful not to perpetuate opposition or rumors of opposition within the mishpochah because in doing so we only end up opposing ourselves and the purposes of God.

There is an ironic story of two Jews who were shipwrecked and cast away on an island that would sustain life. They got together and built houses so each had his own. They even built a little house on the other side of the island as a vacation house. Since they saw themselves as being different kinds of Jews, one built a synagogue the way he wanted a synagogue to be and the other built one another way. Then they built a third synagogue which they reasoned was necessary since it would be the synagogue they could both refuse to attend.

Dear mishpochah, there is a world of difference between

being unique and being separate. We can be unique in the midst of people who are different from us without having to distance ourselves from them. Perhaps some of our mishpochah are so eager to maintain uniqueness that they are falling into the trap of separatism. There is a very natural tendency to identify what makes us unique at the expense of what makes us similar.

Regardless of how we may differ from one another, our "prime directive" is to be more like Jesus. That is enough to keep most of us occupied. And it's something that we all need to encourage one another to do. **Remember, the most powerful distinctive of the gospel is how it serves to unite us.**

The fruit of Y'shua's sacrifice is a universal blessing, that wonderful weave of diversity that is the body, the holy congregation. Let us not make the same mistake that some of our Jewish ancestors made. Let us not despise the unity that the Messiah died to establish. We dare not appeal to unbelieving Jewish people by denying or disguising this awesome reality.

Together we are enjoying a feast of righteousness at a table that was laid for us in the finished work of Y'shua. So when we hear a knock at the door, let's refuse to get up and move to another table. Instead, why not pull up a few more chairs? There truly is plenty of room for everyone.

Part Three
Walking Through the Seasons of Life

Messianic Crossroads:
The Question of Marriage

A world-class concert pianist was approached by an admirer after a stunning performance. "I would give my life to play the way you played this evening," declared the adoring fan.
"I have given my life," responded the virtuoso.

Stop and think for a moment: why do we respect individuals who have achieved super excellence? Certainly we admire their accomplishments, but the discipline and the sacrifices these people undertook to make their mark—whether in the arts, science, business or athletics—are just as remarkable.

Anything of great value can only be achieved at great cost. And it is the cost that underscores the value of any personal achievement. "Wait a minute," you say, "I thought this was an article about messianic marriage! What does *this* have to do with messianic marriage?" It has everything to do with messianic marriage because choices regarding relationships always cost something.

One of the greatest hazards to any relationship, particularly marriage, is failure to count that cost. That failure devalues our choices and allows us to treat our commitments lightly. Too often we come to the table of marriage eager to satisfy ourselves, looking for the most appetizing selection to feed our hungry hearts. If we are disappointed we conclude that something must be wrong with the food, when in reality our own appetites and attitudes are to blame.

Relationships fail and marriages fail because people relate and marry for what they can get instead of what they can give. At the table of marriage, satisfaction comes only through the costly choice of service and self-sacrifice. This principle of **service** is the key, not only to marriage but to messianic lifestyle.

"The Son of Man did not come to be served, but to serve, and to give His life a ransom for many" (Matthew 20:28).

If **service is the key principle**, the first choice is to remain single! Those of us who are married and who knew the Lord while we were still single can attest to the fact that no one has more freedom to focus or more flexibility to serve God than single people. They can do it without shirking responsibilities to spouses or children. That doesn't mean we aren't happy to be married! But let us be the first to respect and affirm anyone who chooses to remain single and to exercise their freedom to serve the Lord.

As mishpochah we need to carefully consider the issue of singleness. We should encourage those who make that kind of sacrifice to the glory of God, yet we often shy away from thinking about this issue because it seems foreign to Jewish culture. So, celibacy is only for priests and nuns?

The Hebrew Scriptures ascribe sacred significance to the marriage relationship. The rabbis understood this and have referred to marriage as *kiddushin* (sanctification). Yet in sanctifying marriage, they went far beyond what the Scriptures say and wrongly condemned celibacy or singleness through such pronunciations as:

"Any man who has no wife lives without joy, without blessing, and without goodness" (Yebamoth 62b).

"Every man is obliged to marry in order to fulfill the duty of procreation, and whoever is not engaged in propagating the race is as if he shed blood, diminishing the Divine image and causing His Presence to depart from Israel" (*Shulhan Arukh*, Even ha-Ezer 1:1).[1]

And yet as is often the case in the Talmud,[2] there is a contradictory or mitigating opinion, from a "patron saint of celibacy," Simeon ben Azzai. Commenting on his own singleness, he declared, "My soul is in love with the Torah; the world can be carried on by others" (Yebamoth 63b). This perspective is actually closer to what we find in the New Testament.

Y'shua sanctified and even encouraged the choice to remain single, first by his own example and second, by declaring that some remain single "for the kingdom of heaven's sake. He who is able to accept it, let him accept it" (Matthew 19:12b). We

---

1. *Encyclopedia Judaica,* "Celibacy," 5:269.

2. Talmud: literally "research"; ancient writings that are a compilation of Jewish oral law, legend and interpretation of the Scriptures; they are considered divinely inspired as the "perpetuation" of Torah by religious Jews; the compilation of the Talmud had come to an end by the sixth century, but the commentaries and addenda have continued.

should not presume that if glandular and emotional impulses are left unmet, they will leave us miserable and unfulfilled.

The Apostle Paul affirms the choice of singleness in the seventh chapter of 1 Corinthians, even preferring it to the choice of marriage. Some critics have charged that Paul was influenced by a Hellenistic dualism—Greek philosophy that taught that spirit is good and flesh is evil; therefore marriage and physical relationships are bad while singleness and celibacy are good. This is a flagrant twisting of the text. Paul never condemned marriage but clearly explained that his preference for **singleness** was based upon the principle of service to God.

"But I want you to be without care. He who is unmarried cares for the things of the Lord—how he may please the Lord. But he who is married cares about the things of the world—how he may please his wife" (1 Corinthians 7:32-33).

Paul never said that those who marry cannot serve the Lord. He advised that some people may choose not to marry so that they may give their undistracted attention in service to God. A choice like that costs something. As family, we must learn to value and affirm those who make that choice and recognize it as a gift from God.

We may not openly demean singleness as the Talmud does. Yet other subtle and not-so-subtle ways of undermining single brothers and sisters abound. There are unsolicited attempts at "matchmaking." There are attitudes and even sermons that suggest a person does not really grow to maturity, understand the meaning of commitment or experience fulfillment until married. Let's refrain from discouraging the godly choice of singleness. Let's affirm the principle of service and those who make costly choices to the glory of God.

While the principle of service leads only a few to make an actual commitment to be single, it nevertheless causes many more to remain single by limiting their scope of possible marriage partners. These are people who might have chosen to be married, but instead remained single. None of the potential partners they met were building the kind of lives that would enable them to continue in the kind of service to which they believe God called them. This is true for both genders. One can easily see the point illustrated: a woman is established in ministry. She knows that a husband who is not equally committed to ministry could decide on a move that would isolate her from the particular work she is called to do.

Still others might have been so preoccupied with their service to God in their youth that one day they wake up to find that years have passed and they are alone—without the kind of marriage prospects they once had. They don't regret how they spent their younger years, but they never made an official commitment to remaining single either. They don't complain or consider themselves cheated; yet there is a certain ache—a wistfulness and admission to close friends that they sometimes miss having a spouse and children.

While these people may not have consciously committed to staying single, their priorities in serving God cost them the same as if they had decided never to marry. These also deserve our affirmation and respect—the recognition that they paid a high price in order to serve God in the particular way to which they were called.

Therefore, my first and strongest affirmation is to those who have remained single for the sake of their service to God.

My second affirmation is to Jewish believers who commit themselves to marrying other Jewish believers because they believe that God has called them to do so. The cost is a considerably smaller "marriage pool."

Sometimes these Jewish believers must wait longer than they would like before marrying; sometimes they might close their eyes to possibilities that would be very attractive had they not made this commitment. It is easier to find loving and accepting mates who are Gentile believers on the basis of sheer numbers. The more difficult choice is for the Jewish believer to find another messianic Jew.

You can tell those who have counted the cost of that choice because they do not constantly complain that there are not enough "eligible" Jewish believers. **If a commitment is to the Lord, there is no bitterness or resentment over the high price of that commitment.** Those who pay the price for that kind of commitment should be affirmed and not judged.

Some have questioned the motives of these people while others have gone so far as to pronounce that such a commitment is wrong, prejudiced and insulting to our Gentile brothers and sisters. I would not want to be in the position of making such a pronouncement!

I can't help but wonder if those who do pass judgment might not be a little defensive. Some people view others' commitments through a lens labeled, "What does this say about me?" That is a short-sighted and insensitive lens. The result is that not only do these people fail to give the support others need, but they also fail to receive support because they wrongly suppose that people are slighting them.

My wife Patti is not Jewish, yet I admire and respect my friends who have limited their choices of possible mates to Jewish believers. Their commitment to "marry Jewish" is not an indictment of my marriage nor anyone else's. I am grateful to be blessed with my wonderful family, but our personal happiness does not change my opinion that marriages between two Jewish believers are desirable for a number of reasons.

Such marriages contribute to the continuity of the Jewish people as a whole and, more specifically, to the believing Jewish remnant. We are encountering a growing number of people who lay claim to a Jewish heritage that doesn't appear valid upon any kind of inquiry. There is the individual who tells you he is Jewish and upon further explanation you discover that through "research," he discovered that one of his great-grandparents was Jewish. By what standard can we consider this person a Jew?

Or think of this scenario that may be closer to home: that children of a Jewish/Gentile believing couple are raised with a sense of their Jewishness. Perhaps there is even a nearby messianic congregation they attend while growing up. What happens if one of the children marries a Gentile believer? What will be their children's claim to Jewish identity? This is a particularly touchy issue—I know because I may be facing it myself someday. Patti and I work hard to provide our children with a strong Jewish identity. Yet, if our children marry Gentiles, how much of a claim to Jewishness will our grandchildren have, given that I would be the only Jewish grandparent?

We may have the conviction to raise our children Jewish with the full participation of a Gentile spouse. Yet we cannot guarantee the conviction of our children if they marry Gentiles, nor of their children, if the Lord tarries.

I am saddened whenever I meet a person with Jewish background who has walked away from any involvement in things Jewish. I feel it is a great loss when Jewish believers fail to identify with the remnant.

Now the fact is that God will ultimately preserve us as a people, but that does not mean that we have no responsibility to preserve our own heritage and unique witness. God invites us to participate in the preservation of our people and our heritage, not abandon it (1 Corinthians 7:17-18). We ought to encourage and affirm Jewish believers who feel that God has called them to reinforce and preserve their heritage in a way that requires them to marry only a Jewish believer.

Another consideration is more mundane, but in some cases it can cause significant trouble in a marriage: cultural differences. There is tremendous pressure mitigating against marriage these days; we live in a world that is constantly undermining the idea of absolute commitment to anything. With all the given difficulties inherent in any marriage, partners of Jewish-Gentile marriages might encounter further difficulties that are not easily resolved.

The Jewish partner needs to realize that at some point he or she may have to deal with feelings of guilt for "marrying out." That is not to say that such guilt is justified! Yet, inherent in most Jewish upbringing is the idea that Jews should marry Jews. Anyone contemplating intermarriage should take an honest look at themselves and evaluate whether they are prepared to deal with cultural differences in a godly way. Precious little good it will do your spouse if you quote all the Scripture verses to say that Jews and Gentiles are one in Messiah, and then make disparaging remarks about "Gentile food" or "pagan traditions" that were a cherished part of your mate's childhood.

Obviously the right and godly thing for us to do is not disparage one another at all! But let's be honest and admit that we are still in the *process* of becoming more like the Messiah. None of us is as sensitive to people's feelings as Y'shua is. Don't saddle a spouse with having to live with you while you work on becoming more accepting of his or her background.

The same can be true of a prospective Gentile spouse who doesn't really have much appreciation for Jewish culture. When the honeymoon is over, you don't want to find yourself married to someone who complains to his or her friends about "having to put up with pushy Jewish in-laws."

Such things ought not to be among believers, but sanctification is a process. Ethnic pride can creep into relationships in very subtle ways and can be very hurtful. It is not that we should condone or make room for these wrong attitudes. But we should consider the possibility that they might exist and not put others in a position to be hurt by them.

In the same vein, it is important to remember that when people marry, it is not merely a knitting together of two individuals—it is also a joining of families. Though God's approval should always be first and foremost in any marriage, the parents of the bride and groom are not out of the picture. We cannot order our lives to please unbelieving Jewish parents, for if that were the case, most parents would settle for nothing less than a renunciation of our faith. And yet, there are matters where we can take their feelings and sensitivities into account without violating our calling.

Marriage to a godly Gentile partner is absolutely acceptable in God's sight, but if your family sees it as a rejection of everything Jewish, you might choose not to exercise your liberty for their sake. I know one Gentile believer who married a Jewish believer but strongly advocates Jewish believers marrying one another—in large part, for the sake of the in-laws. This means thinking things through, taking others into consideration and making decisions before emotional attachments occur.

A similar reason for affirming Jewish-Jewish marriages is that of maintaining a testimony to the Jewish community. Marrying a Jewish believer can be one way of telling the Jewish community, "what matters to you matters to me too."

Whether we feel the pros and cons of intermarriage apply to us, we should recognize that many people consider intermarriage one of the Jewish community's most pressing problems. According to Richard J. Israel, director of B'nai B'rith in Boston, Massachusetts, "There are few phenomena of Jewish life today that cause as much angry debate and pain and bewilderment as intermarriage."[3]

According to a study done at Brandeis University, the national intermarriage rate was at 29 percent with some areas of the country showing as high as a 40 percent intermarriage rate. A national population study commissioned by the Council of Jewish Federations gives an even more dramatic statistic. According to their report, 49 percent of all Jews who have married since 1985 have non-Jewish spouses. Other reports bring that figure to 52 percent. The plethora of articles and studies demonstrates the level of concern the Jewish community feels over the intermarriage issue and specifically, the fear of assimilation.

When a Jewish believer makes the effort to find another Jewish believer as a spouse, that makes a statement.

But let's remember in messianic marriages, we are dealing with the principle of service—and it is God whom we serve in maintaining a testimony, not ourselves or the Jewish community. We must be careful to distinguish between maintaining a testimony and seeking acceptance. A testimony is a statement. That statement does not necessarily make us acceptable in the eyes of those to whom we are testifying! It is their responsibility to decide whether to deal with our testimony. And we must remember that the acceptance we seek is not for ourselves, but for Y'shua.

I would caution those who choose to marry other Jewish believers as a testimony to examine their hearts and their hopes very carefully. The commitment to marry a Jewish believer is indeed a valid statement and might be the right one for you to make, but if by making that statement you think that either you or the gospel will gain approval in the Jewish community, think again.

The Central Conference of American Rabbis (Reform

---

3. *Third Jewish Catalogue,* compiled and edited by Michael Strassfeld and Sharon Strassfeld, the Jewish Publications Society of America (Philadephia) 1980, p. 254.

Judaism) dealt with the question of whether a Reform rabbi is allowed to marry a messianic Jew to an unbelieving Jew. Though the Reform Jewish movement is perhaps the most liberal of all, the answer was still no, "Unless the messianic Jew renounces his belief in Jesus of Nazareth and becomes a Jew rather than a messianic Jew, we must consider him a Christian and cannot officiate at his marriage. . . . We should be much stricter in our relationship with 'messianic Jews' than with Christians. . . . We should do everything in our power. . . . to maintain a strict separation of anyone connected with this group."[4]

When the official response of the most liberal body within Judaism declares that a marriage of a Jew to a messianic Jew is worse than intermarriage, what kind of acceptance can we possibly hope for? But stop and think about it. We know that we don't have to choose between being Jewish and believing in Jesus. But if the rabbis were right and we did have to choose, I hope that each and every one of us would choose Jesus!

Returning to the commitment of some who choose to marry only Jewish believers—we should encourage and foster a community that upholds people who have made difficult choices. That means supporting Jewish believers who commit to marrying other Jewish believers on the basis of what they feel God has asked of them. Some in the mishpochah need to turn away from a "reverse prejudice" that demands that a Jewish believer be willing to marry a Gentile believer in order to prove he or she is not a bigot or a spiritually insensitive person.

Do not misinterpret my first two affirmations as a condemnation of those who have chosen a third option. Because finally, we should affirm the sanctity of any marriage between two believers in Jesus who are seeking to please Him. That means affirming marriages between Jewish and Gentile believers as well. In God's grace, such marriages can be a reflection of the diversity found in the body of Christ.

What is a messianic marriage? It is a marriage where each partner is determined to serve the Messiah. Now if Jews were the

---

4. Collected Response of the Conference of American Rabbis, edited by Walter Jacob, Central Conference of American Rabbis Publication, New York, 1983, pp. 471-74 passim.

only servants of the Messiah, then Jewish believers would be obligated to marry only other Jewish believers. But the body of Christ is diverse; therefore, we can affirm all believing marriages, whether Jewish, Gentile or mixed. Let no one then discourage or undermine a marriage between Jewish and Gentile Christians.

> Therefore remember that you, once Gentiles in the flesh— who are called Uncircumcision by what is called the Circumcision made in the flesh by hands—that at that time you were without Christ, being aliens from the common- wealth of Israel and strangers from the covenants of promise, having no hope and without God in the world. But now in Christ Jesus you who once were far off have been brought near by the blood of Christ. For He Himself is our peace, who has made both one, and has broken down the middle wall of separation. Now, therefore, you are no longer strangers and foreigners, but fellow citizens with the saints and members of the household of God. (Ephesians 2:11-14, 19)

In both testaments, the prohibition regarding "intermarriage" is for religious, not racial purposes. In the Hebrew Scriptures, we read that Jewish people were to remain separate because whenever we mixed in with the nations, we fell into idolatry and strayed from faith in the God of Israel. The Scriptures also show exceptions in such notable examples as Moses' wives and of course, Ruth the Moabitess. Furthermore, the New Testament describes a breaking down of barriers between Jews and Gentiles, which was only dimly foreshadowed in the story of Ruth.

The best marriages are those in which both people think things through and consider their service to Y'shua as the first item of business in their relationship. That is why God com- manded us to contemplate marriage only with those who are also followers of the Savior: "Do not be unequally yoked together with unbelievers. For what fellowship has righteousness with lawlessness? And what communion has light with darkness?" (2 Corinthians 6:14).

The marriages that present the most difficult problems are those patterned after society's bent ideals and expectations instead of what the Bible says. It is tragic when people in the messianic community marry for wrong reasons or with wrong expectations. Those marriages tend to disintegrate and dissolve in the same way that those outside the messianic community do, because the spouses failed to realize that God never intended marriage to be a self-serving relationship. They failed to follow the principle of service.

Whether married or single, Jewish or Gentile, if our first consideration is how we can best serve God, then surely our lives and our relationships will be pleasing to God, a testimony to the Jewish community and to the whole world. Our leadership (and in fact the messianic community as a whole) is responsible to foster the kind of teaching and pastoral care that promotes biblical standards and godly relationships. These matters are not solely private concerns, inasmuch as they greatly reflect the character and conduct of our movement. We dare not wring our hands over assimilation, bad marriages or unhealthy relations between singles if we have failed to provide the proper education, guidance and care.

We also should challenge one another to count the cost and make hard decisions concerning marriage. Paul's words in 1 Corinthians took on a particular urgency because of the time and the situation in which believers were living.

> But this I say, brethren, the time is short, so that from now on even those who have wives should be as though they had none, those who weep as though they did not weep, those who rejoice as though they did not rejoice, those who buy as though they did not possess, and those who use this world as not misusing it. For the form of this world is passing away. (1 Corinthians 7:29-31)

We live in times that are not altogether unlike the time in which Paul wrote. The eschatological urgency that he conveyed in that passage should provide perspective for those who have not yet made marital commitments. The apostle was not trying to be a spoilsport, but rather he explains his advice:

> And this I say for your own profit, not that I may put a leash on you, but for what is proper, and that you may

serve the Lord without distraction. (1 Corinthians 7:35)

There again is the principle of undistracted devotion to the Lord. For many, if not most, the choice to remain single is too great a burden to bear. No one should feel guilty for marrying or desiring to marry a suitable believer!

But whether you are married, plan to be married, would like to be married but don't know if you ever will be, or have decided to remain single, there is one hope we hold in common. We all await the greatest messianic marriage of all. Through faith in the Messiah of Israel, Jews and Gentiles—married and single alike—have been arrayed in the robes of Y'shua's righteousness. We await Him as His bride adorned for His coming. We look forward to the great marriage supper of the Lamb. There we will rejoice in the unity He has given us with each other and in the eternal life that we will share together with Him. Let's wait with undistracted devotion.

An Age-Old Challenge

Growing old is no joy, but Pearl Weinberg hadn't realized how awful it could be until the death of her beloved Jacob. Two years had passed, yet she often forgot Jacob was gone and set the table for two or bought herring (which she had never liked!) because it was a favorite of his.

It wasn't just Jacob that she missed. She missed what she was when he was still alive—she missed being his wife. What was more, with "Dad" gone, it was getting more and more difficult for Pearl to see herself as "Mom." Pearl was grateful that she could depend on her son and daughter-in-law, but she would have preferred to be able to be "doing for them" rather than needing them to "do" for her. Her own children still called her Ma, but it was her daughter-in-law Sheila who still had children to raise, and Pearl had to remember that when the little ones called for Ma, they didn't mean her.

Pearl's son and daughter-in-law's house had become the center of family activities. Not that Gordon and Sheila weren't good to her, and Pearl knew that Sheila welcomed her company and her help. But it felt strange to be an assistant in Sheila's kitchen instead of the chief cook and bottle-washer in her own.

Pearl also found that many things she used to enjoy had become difficult. She loved reading and used to buy a new novel every week, but now the words blurred and she had to strain to read them. "Why do they have to make the print so small?" she wondered.

She had always loved to socialize, but it was harder to get out since the doctor had said, "No driving at night." Pearl hated to impose on others by asking them to squire her around. So many who would have helped or been companions were gone. Visiting those who were sitting *shiva*[1] had become an all-too-frequent part of her social calendar.

When she did manage to get out, it was difficult to sit in a

---

1. *Shiva:* a seven-day period of mourning for the dead during which close relatives of the deceased cover all the mirrors in the house, stay home, wear no shoes and receive condolence visits from friends and relatives.

room full of people, smiling and pretending to be part of the conversation when she caught only faint syllables in the midst of whispers. Others seemed content to let her sit quietly, even though she had always been a lively conversationalist. Those who did notice how quiet she was attributed it to the loss of her husband rather than the loss of her hearing and assumed she would once again begin talking and laughing—when she was ready. Ignoring her less-than-sociable behavior seemed the polite thing to do.

Pearl had finally sold the house that she and Jacob had shared for forty years. She knew she'd made a sensible, even a necessary move, but she missed her three-bedroom, two-bathroom house with the patio. Some of the plants she had given away, but she watched many turn yellow and wither because they could not grow in the apartment.

Keepsakes she had cherished seemed to crowd each other out in the new flat. She never imagined that such a nice place could be so crowded and yet so lonely. She had packed carefully, but cardboard boxes could not hold what was dearest to her—and what they did hold was more than could fit into her freshly painted, thin-walled little apartment. Sure, there were plenty of mirrors to make the place *look* bigger. In fact, there were too many mirrors. Everywhere Pearl looked, she was confronted with the reflection of some old woman who had managed to trap her soul.

Gordon and Sheila sat quietly together in the front room, the silence between them occasionally broken by the barking of a neighbor's dog. Their minds raced back and forth between past experiences and present problems. What were they going to do? It seemed that since they lost Dad, Ma was going downhill fast. There were so many questions to answer, so many problems to be solved.

What would be wrong with fixing up the spare bedroom? Gordon thought. After all, his mother had given so much of her life to raise him. He couldn't bear visiting her in that small, sterile apartment, hearing her talk about Dad like he was still alive. It seemed like everything had come to a halt for his mother when Dad died. She didn't seem to be able to make herself part of anything that was happening now.

Surrounded by a loving family, maybe she would be able to cope better with the loss they all felt. At least, Gordon hoped so. Besides, the tumble she'd taken in the bathtub last week had shaken him. Fortunately, Ma was only bruised, but what if she'd broken her hip with no one there to help her? He felt it was wrong for her to be alone. After all, hadn't she always been there when he needed her? The children would love having Grandma around. Maybe it would even take some of the burden off Sheila—help her to get out more and have more time to herself.

Sheila loved the fact that Gordon was a good son. And she got along far better with Pearl than most of her friends did with their in-laws. Still, to have Ma move in—after all, Ma did like to be in charge, especially in the kitchen. And then there were the kids to consider. It seemed like Ma spent half the time instructing Sheila on how to discipline the kids, while the other half she spent spoiling them!

Sheila had always found a good balance between accepting her mother-in-law's advice on some occasions and firmly standing up to her on others. Now, with Ma failing, she didn't know if she could continue to draw the line. It's one thing to tell a loved one to mind her own business. It's another thing to tell a loved one who is grief stricken and ill to mind her own business. If Ma did move in, Sheila would want her to feel at home, of course. But would it be possible to make her feel at home without letting her take over? Sheila chided herself for being so selfish.

The Weinbergs looked at each other and Gordon spoke for both of them, "What are we going to do about Ma?"

Perhaps the problems of the Weinberg family are very real to you, whether you are facing them now or thinking of the future. Even if the Weinbergs' situation seems a long way off, realize that if the Messiah tarries and if God grants you a long life, *you will one day face the aging of a loved one and ultimately your own aging.* What's more, in the community of believers we have mishpochah who are dealing with these problems on a daily basis, and we all need to concern ourselves with these family matters.

The problems and challenges of aging involve a number of

people, including unbelievers. Imagine the tensions that could arise in the Weinberg scenario if Pearl were a believer but Gordon and Sheila were not, or if Gordon and Sheila were believers and Pearl was not. Few Jewish believers are so fortunate as to have believing parents and believing adult children.

Whether your role is believing parent or child to an unbelieving family, the key to responding appropriately to the difficulties of aging is to understand the process, determine a godly perspective and then plan, inasmuch as it is possible, how to respond accordingly.

The Aging Process

"The rocks have grown tall, the near have become distant, two have turned into three, and the peacemaker of the home has ceased" (Shabbat 152a).[2]

Coping with aging means coping with many losses. The process of coping with these losses is known as grief. Grief does not necessarily begin at the moment that someone or something we hold dear is suddenly torn from us. For many of us, grief begins the moment we realize that we are going to lose someone or something that we hold dear. But whenever it begins, grief changes us. It causes us to re-evaluate who we are in light of the missing piece or pieces of our lives.

Losing a loved one is not the only cause of grief. People who are divorced, people who wanted to marry but didn't, people who found they could not have children and people who are disabled through illness or accident are just a few examples of people experiencing grief. In other words, the loss of a person's *role*—be it a role they actually had or one fervently hoped for—is a very real cause of grief. The loss of health, independence, influence, the loss of being protected or nurtured by parents who now need protection and nurture, each of these things requires the painful acceptance, adjustment and reorientation that a grieving person must undergo.

Still, the most difficult blow of aging will usually be the death

---

2. This saying of Simeon B. Halafta is explained to mean, "I have grown old, even those near are as difficult to visit as those at a distance, my two legs need an additional stick for walking and I can no longer exercise a man's functions."

of a loved one. That terrifying experience is a shock regardless of whether it was expected. And it is compounded as not only spouses but sisters, brothers, friends and co-workers all approach their final years together. They pass out of the aging person's life one by one, some so quickly and unexpectedly that the bereaved can't help wondering who will be the next to go.

As we age, it seems like we have fewer and fewer choices. Some of us will not be able to maintain control of our own bodies; others of us will find that our minds seem to have a will and a destination of their own. Unless we remain focused on the Lord, a cloud of intellectual and spiritual impotence can settle around us and dampen all our dreams for the future.

Adult children who see what is happening to their aging parents will also have feelings of denial and anger associated with their parents' grief. Moreover, they will probably begin their own grieving process, realizing the relatively short time they have left with their own parent or parents. They may well begin to grieve over their own mortality as well. Fearing the painful loss that a parent's aging reminds them they will face causes some children to distance themselves from those who need them most. This can turn the already difficult process of aging into a morbid experience.

Adult children often recoil at the role-reversal that is a natural part of life because they are unprepared. Helplessness to prevent the suffering of parents who were always there to ease their children's pain can cause those grown children to become frightened and angry. Some feel terribly lonely and vulnerable when faced with the responsibility of making decisions for those who once decided everything for them. Many resent their parent(s) for what they perceive as abandonment. They fail to understand and prepare, be it emotionally or financially, for their new responsibilities. Some fail to such an extent that they abandon their parents to the state or to some nursing home that they pay off to keep their parent(s) from becoming an excessive burden, hence the "my children come visit me twice a year" syndrome. That is a crime of which I hope none of us will ever be guilty!

Even when people exercise their responsibility in love, there can be tensions and difficulties. Sometimes when offspring who have children of their own become caretakers of their parents, they feel trapped between the needs and demands of two generations. They might become impatient and irritable with their young children as well as their elderly parents.

Once again, for those whose thoughts are not centered on the Lord, selfishness and its well-deserved accompanying guilt can take over. Thoughts such as, "Is this what I have to look forward to?" mortify the adult children who can scarcely believe they could be so mean as to think of their own comforts at a time when Mom and/or Dad is suffering.

Aging involves grief—adjustments to losses and changing roles—for *all* concerned. A good understanding of grief is crucial to grasping the aging process, whether or not there has been a recent death in the family. Your local bookstore or library will have a selection of books on the subject; it would be helpful for you to choose one if you are not yet familiar with the "grief cycle."

What the Scriptures Say

As believers, we can face our own aging or the aging of our loved ones with the strength and help of God, knowing that He makes the difference. The Lord is our comfort and our joy whatever the circumstance, but what can we know from Scripture about growing old? You may want to do your own study, but here are some points to get you started:

God demands respect and honor for the elderly; when we fulfill that command, we actually show respect for God himself: "You shall rise before the gray headed and honor the presence of an old man and fear your God. I am the LORD" (Leviticus 19:32).

Parents deserve our special respect: "Honor your father and your mother, that your days may be long upon the land which the LORD your God is giving you" (Exodus 20:12).

We are to guard against ingratitude toward aging parents: "Listen to your father who begot you, and do not despise your mother when she is old" (Proverbs 23:22).

In contrast, God is pleased when we show gratitude and take responsibility for the debt that cries out to be paid. To meet that obligation in love shows that we don't just have a say-so faith but a do-so faith: "But if any widow has children or grandchildren, let them first learn to show piety at home and to repay their parents; for this is good and acceptable before God" (1 Timothy 5:4).

Y'shua himself indicated the importance of proper respect and care for aging parents. He pointed to failure to care for parents as one of the worst examples of how man-made piety undermines God's commands: "For God commanded, saying, 'Honor your father and your mother'; and, 'He who curses father or mother, let him be put to death.' But you say, 'Whoever says to his father or mother, "Whatever profit you might have received from me is a gift to God"—then he need not honor his father or mother.' Thus you have made the commandment of God of no effect by your tradition" (Matthew 15:4-6).

Since our Messiah stressed the significance of caring for parents, we need to take the responsibility very seriously indeed. As disciples of Messiah, we must be examples of the generous and loving care God demands.

Leaders and pastors have a special responsibility toward the elderly. Paul instructed the young pastor Timothy to regard the elderly in the body of Christ with the same kindness and respect he would show to members of his own family: "Do not rebuke an older man, but exhort him as a father" (1 Timothy 5:1).

Our Response

God's kingdom accords great dignity to the aging, and we need to regard our own aging process and that of our loved ones with the respect God commands. As messianic believers, we should be examples, not only of how to age gracefully, but also of how to care graciously and respectfully for our aging mishpochah. We ought to plan now, as it is difficult to make decisions and develop attitudes when the need surfaces through some crisis.

What can we do, young and old alike, to reflect God's standards within our community?

For Our Elders . . .

You who are elders should not be content to take a backseat in the community of believers. It is all too easy to feel slighted by the overzealous and sometimes unthinking youth of the messianic movement. We need our elders, whether or not the need is expressed. We need you for the wisdom you can impart to us and for the nurturing you can give to our young children. Many believers in the messianic community did not have the example of Christ-following parents or grandparents. Who will be their examples, their role models of elderly people who love Y'shua?

Nothing brings more cheer to the young than to find "grand-parently" people who can share their joy and enthusiasm and live in the "now" instead of "the days when I was young." It might not always be so easy to bring cheer, but my grandfather, Fred Kendall, had a practice that seemed to work for him. He said that it was important to say five affirmative, happy things for each complaint. By the time you have said five things that are a praise to God, you will have forgotten what there was to complain about.

We also need the elderly in our midst to remind the main-stream Jewish community that they cannot dismiss us as being merely a collection of "young rebels." We are a movement of old and young alike (with the accompanying degrees of maturity) who know and love Y'shua. We need to hear more from our elderly mishpochah!

If your children are believers, you have a right to expect that they will behave toward you in a way that is pleasing to the Lord and honoring to you as their parents. A more difficult situation is when your children are not believers. Do expect them to respect your faith, even if they can't share it. Many unbelieving children are very respectful and caring toward their parents, but if this is not the case, you cannot expect Scripture to carry the same weight it would with children who are believers.

There may be practical concerns with certain unbelieving off-spring. You may be among the minority whose wishes with respect to your faith and finances might be circumvented by children who do not share your concerns or love for the Lord. If you have cause to think that this might happen, it would be wise to take steps to make sure that your wishes are fulfilled. In the case of incapacities due to illness, you would want to make certain that any power of attorney would be in the hands of those who you believe would honor the Lord and your commitment to Him.

Choose someone who will follow through with your wishes with respect to your care, even through to your funeral, burial and the settlement of your estate. For example, should you wish to prepare a word of testimony to be read at your funeral, you want to be certain it will not be "left out" by a well-meaning unbelieving son or daughter.

When it comes to the matter of arranging for death and burial, let's be frank. Often, as Jewish believers, we are refused burial in Jewish cemeteries or the Jewish section of a cemetery. Many of those who insist that we have abandoned the Jewish community are ready to shut us out and then point to the separation as though it was our idea, when in fact it was theirs. Steps can and should be taken to secure the kind of interment you feel is appropriate.

Some messianic groups have taken steps to secure burial plots. If you have not thought of this, perhaps you might speak to your pastor or spiritual leader to see if such arrangements can be made. We need a *chevra kaddish*.[3]

What about witnessing to children and grandchildren who do not yet know the Lord? Most parents have to admit that though they thought so at the time, not everything they taught their children was right or true. If you taught your children that Jesus is not for Jews, now is the time to tell them that you were wrong. At the same time, you should not seek to undermine the authority of your children with respect to their own children.

This is a touchy subject. On the one hand, your children have the right to oversee the religious education of their offspring. On the other hand, you should command enough respect within your family to interact with them on the basis of who you are without covering up what you believe. It is important to maintain your influence within the family structure while also respecting your children's parental authority. For example, if a little one comes to you and says, "Mommy and Daddy say that we're not supposed to believe in Jesus," you might say something like, "Your mom and dad don't believe the same things about Jesus as your *bubbe/zayde* [or whatever the grandchildren call you]. Some day

---

3. *Chevra kaddish:* literally a "holy society." This is actually a burial society for Jewish believers.

when you are old enough you will have to decide for yourself what you believe."

When answering questions about your faith, you can precede your explanations with "I believe . . ." and thus speak the truth in love while acknowledging that the rest of the family may not share your convictions.

For Children of the Aging . . .

We must remember that the verse "honor your father and mother" does not only apply to children who have yet to leave their parents' house and authority. That verse is just as applicable to adults who have left their parents' household long ago. This duty, described as *"kibbud av va-em,"* or honoring of one's parents, should be a primary consideration for those of us who believe in Y'shua. We honor our parents not only by what we say to them, but also by what we say about them. We honor them with our tone of voice as well as with our words. We honor them by appreciating what they have done for us and by doing for them when the time comes.

This brings me to an aside: there are those who try to manipulate Jewish believers with the scriptural mandate to honor our parents. It is true that few unbelieving Jewish parents consider themselves honored by their children's belief in Jesus. Yet if we esteem our parents' wishes more highly than God's, we dishonor Y'shua and yes, even our parents. It may be necessary and right to sacrifice our creature comforts to honor our parents, but it is never right to compromise our commitment to Jesus. Anyone who insists that God's commandment calls for you to keep quiet about your faith is concerned about his or her own agenda, not God's.

As you seek to honor your parents and to cope with the changes that are taking place in their lives, memories become very important. Sit down and take stock of how things have changed; try to view your parents with some balance and perspective. Recall for yourself and for them some of the good times and some of the hard times you've weathered together.

If one or both of your parents become unable to care for themselves, you will have to answer the question of how to meet their physical needs. It is a shame to you if you have comfort while your parents' needs are unmet. (One messianic leader, in pre-marital counseling sessions, tells prospective mates that they should be ready to give 20 percent of their income toward the care of their in-laws if necessary. If both sets of parents need help, that's a possible 40 percent of the couple's income.)

If you have siblings, this is a time to draw together. Caring for aging parents is a privilege and a responsibility that should be shared. Make a list of your parents' needs. Discuss who can meet those needs and how. Remember that unless your parents are incapable of participating, it should never be presumed that the rest of the family "knows what is best" for them. The younger generation needs to be strong and capable without depriving the elderly of their dignity and their right to make choices.

Many people automatically assume that the only right thing to do is to take their parents into their home. That may be the best answer in some cases, but it is not necessarily right in all cases. For some, having a live-in parent could create marriage problems that would be difficult to solve. For others, it might also seriously strain the relationship with their parent(s). There may not be adequate space to ensure comfort and privacy for all concerned. Some people might be able to modify their home or find a new one, but that is not always possible.

If any of these things would constitute a problem, you need to take steps to provide as much outside help as possible. There are many support services that can be secured, such as cleaning, transportation, meals, part-or full-time nursing, etc. You have to be willing to consider solutions that you may not like. A resource that you might find helpful is a book titled *You and Your Aging Parent* by Barbara Silverstone and Helen Kandel Hyman, published by Pantheon.

Whatever decision you make with respect to your parents, you must make sure that you see the issues clearly. Often, children are motivated by their need for parental approval or fear of rejection, both of which we carry with us throughout our lives.

If your parents are not believers then, of course, your most important motivation should be concern for their spiritual well-being. If they happen to be unsympathetic or angry about your belief in Y'shua, you still owe them the same care.

It is all too easy to be cynical about your parents making a decision for the Lord. After all, you have known them all your life and you know how closed they have been to the gospel in the past. You wonder how they could ever believe! Just remember that it is never too late for anyone to make a decision for the Lord. Abraham and Sarah were certainly senior citizens when they began to follow the Lord (Genesis 12:4), which is something you might point out to your parents when they try to tell you that they are too old to change their ways.

If you have children, do not try to keep them quiet about the Lord when your folks are around. Grandchildren are wonderful messengers of the gospel. As they learn to love the Lord, they might well recite Scripture verses or sing songs about Y'shua to your parents. You might need to console your children if your parents respond negatively. On the other hand, do not be surprised if your parents will hear from your children what they won't hear from you. Never give up hope. Never allow yourself to become so cynical that you give up praying for them and witnessing to them for Jesus. Every single year some of our parents discover new life in Y'shua. Maybe this year it will be your parents!

If your parents are believers, then look to involve them in as much activity in the local congregation as possible. Give them chances to tell Bible stories, to help your children with Scripture memory and to remind them that their future is secure in the Lord. Our congregations and fellowship groups need to strike a balance between giving opportunities for leadership to the young and giving a place of honor and influence to our elders.

Whether or not your aging loved ones know the Lord, your care and concern can help them through this crucial time.

For Young and Old

Let's remember that while death and disease are part of the fall (and not what God created us for), aging is a part of life that God has blessed and hallowed and honored. Let's look for ways to reflect God's desire to honor those who are aging and to honor

Him as we age. Do we not have His promise that aging is not a descent into twilight ending in darkness? Getting old can be a joy because God makes every day new, and one day soon He will make you new . . . in body, mind and spirit. Get ready!

The Facts of Death

Some believe that we Jewish believers in Jesus have merely added our faith in Him as an extension of Judaism. This is not true! Our faith in Y'shua has made us different from our fellow Jews in many ways, and those differences are not trivial. They are matters of life and death.

I was too close to the edge! I tried to veer away but stumbled on a rock and was suddenly over the cliff. I grabbed for something, anything, to break my fall, but there was only the rush of air as I plummeted down, down, down. I wanted to scream but could not. My whole body tensed—and I awoke with a start.

Maybe you know the terror of such dreams and the relief of awakening. But if you have already experienced tragedy, you know that death is not just for dreams, television or the cinema. Death and dying are as real as life itself.

Death is that ugly intruder who comes to tear soul and body asunder. There is no beauty in a corpse. A skilled mortician might create a pleasant illusion, but human beings have an inherent sense that a body no longer animated by a soul is somehow obscene. There is an inner nakedness that causes some to stare and others to avert their eyes.

Our media is saturated with violence and images of death, yet on a personal level most people exclude the subject from conversation. Death is a ubiquitous enemy, but we anesthetize ourselves to its painful presence. People keep thoughts and fears about death to themselves in a conspiracy of silence. Even believers may try to ignore the fact of death or postpone thinking about it, but eventually death lays claim to each of us and to those we love.

The good news is, we don't have to be afraid!

Y'shua came to "release those who through fear of death were all their lifetime subject to bondage" (Hebrews 2:15). Fear of death causes bondage, but Jesus has liberated us. We need not be part of the conspiracy of silence. We have a hope that is unlike that of the rest of the world. For us, death is but a door through which we pass into the presence of our Lord. We have confidence in our eternal relationship with God through Y'shua. We

will be united with Him and reunited with those we love in the
Lord who have gone before us.

Whereas fear of death subjects people to bondage, con-
fronting death liberates and produces something of great value.
"The days of our lives are seventy years; and if by reason of
strength they are eighty years, yet their boast is only labor and
sorrow; for it is soon cut off, and we fly away. . . . So teach us to
number our days, that we may gain a heart of wisdom" (Psalm
90:10, 12).

It is time for us, as mishpochah, to speak frankly and to help
one another face the facts of mortality so that by God's grace we
may gain that heart of wisdom. Wisdom will help us recognize
realities and overcome temptations in matters of life and death.

Unbelievers Do Not Share Our Hope

This is a harsh reality, but it is better to endure reality and act
accordingly than to be lulled into passivity by an illusion.

Most unbelievers know that they do not have hope. My father
tells the story of the funeral of his father, Nathan. Cancer had
claimed Nathan's life at an early age, but he, his wife (my
grandma), my father and his brother had all become believers just
days before his death. At the graveside, my great-grandma was
overcome by the loss of her son. Wailing and crying, she moaned
in Yiddish, "Oh my Nathan, he's in the ground, he's in the
ground. Oh my Nathan, he's in the ground."

My grandma spoke softly through her tears to reply, "No,
Mama, Nathan is not in the ground; he is in heaven with the
Lord." What a contrast. Had my grandfather died a few days ear-
lier, his wife would have had no hope to share with his mother.

This contrast does not exist merely on an ordinary personal
level. The unbeliever's uncertainty about the hereafter is woven
into the very fabric of Judaism. Compare and contrast the words
of two first-century rabbis.

First, hear from one who knew Y'shua: "For this corruptible
must put on incorruption, and this mortal must put on immortality. . . . Then shall be brought to pass the saying that is written:
'Death is swallowed up in victory. O Death, where is your sting?
O Hades, where is your victory?'" (1 Corinthians 15:53-55).

That same rabbi, Saul of Tarsus, also wrote that he was hard pressed to say whether he preferred life or death. He was eager to depart this world and be with the Messiah, but he knew his death would leave a void among the living. Paul did not fear death; in fact he had to curb his desire for death in order to fulfill his responsibilities to younger believers who needed him.[1] He had full confidence in his eternal destiny as well as the eternal destiny of all believers.[2]

Compare Paul's thinking to that of the first-century rabbi who was the architect of modern-day Judaism and who did not know Y'shua:

> When Rabbi Johanan ben Zakkai fell ill, his disciples went in to visit him. When he saw them he began to weep. His disciples said to him, "Lamp of Israel, pillar of the right hand, mighty hammer! Wherefore weepest thou?" He replied, "If I were being taken today before a human king who is here today and tomorrow in the grave, whose anger if he is angry with me does not last forever, who if he imprisons me does not imprison me forever and who if he puts me to death does not put me to everlasting death, and whom I can persuade with words and bribe with money, even so I would weep. Now that I am being taken before the supreme King of Kings, the Holy One, blessed be He who lives and endures forever and ever, whose anger, if He is angry with me, is an everlasting anger, who if He imprisons me imprisons me forever, who if He puts me to death puts me to death forever, and whom I cannot persuade with words or bribe with money—nay more, when there are two ways before me, one leading to Paradise and the other to *Gehinnom*,[3] and I do not know by which I shall be taken, shall I not weep?"[4]

The pious Rabbi Johanan ben Zakkai profoundly articulated

---

1. Philippians 1:21, 23.
2. 2 Timothy 4:7-8.
3. *Gehinnom:* the place of the dead; hell; named after the valley of Hinnom near Jerusalem where idol worshipers offered children on the altars of false gods.
4. Berachot 28b.

the uncertainty, the terror, that death holds for those who have not accepted the reconciling work of the Messiah, Jesus.

Likewise most contemporary rabbis do not speak with such certainty regarding everlasting life and death. Nor do they speak of a personal God who judges and determines eternal destiny. The frequent omission of statements about a God to whom we're accountable or the eternal destiny that awaits us is part of the anesthetization that keeps people from a proper fear. That is, a fear that tells them to concern themselves with God's requirements. (After all, the Scriptures teach that the fear of the Lord is the beginning of wisdom.) But what has not changed since the first century is the unbeliever's statement, "I do not know . . ."

As believers in Jesus we are set apart by our hope. That hope springs from true faith in God's provision, Y'shua, *through whom we can and do know our destiny.* Those who do not share the faith do not share our hope or our destiny. Without that faith and that hope people are terrified of death.

Many try to deny their terror by saying that all paths lead to God. They do not realize how very correct they are! All paths do lead to God. One path leads to Him as Father and Savior; the rest lead to Him as Judge. This adds great urgency to our obligation to tell others—especially our loved ones—of our hope in Jesus. A heart of wisdom recognizes that those who don't know the Messiah do not share our hope and that we have limited opportunities to offer them the hope we have in Jesus.

None of Us Knows How Much Time We Have

My pastor, Scott Rubin, has a heart of wisdom. He knows more about life and death than most other men in their late thirties. If he doesn't think something is worth his time, he'll let you know—sometimes rather bluntly. But he always has time to pray, to pick up a weary traveler at the airport, to encourage a member of his congregation. He knows just how he wants to invest his time and his emotions. He is well past the tenth year of life as a heart transplant survivor. Every day he takes drugs to restrain his immune system from mounting an attack on his heart. We hope and pray that he is with us for many more years, and I am sure he hopes the same. Meanwhile Pastor Scott makes each day count.

Any crisis can be productive if we respond by "numbering our days" and using them to full advantage. But we should not await a crisis to confront our mortality and gain wisdom in the use of our time.

Whether we expect it sooner or later, the fact of death should stimulate us to renewed vigor as we tell those who don't know Messiah about our hope in Him. We have no idea how long we will be around to tell it, just as we do not know how long they will be around to hear. Physical death always looms larger than spiritual death, yet which should concern us more? In the grand scheme of things, spiritual death is far more significant. *Yet it is physical death that makes the condition of spiritual death permanent.*

Our own death may seem of little concern when compared to the death of loved ones who don't know the Lord. Perhaps no grief is as profound as that of losing close friends or relatives who have refused the gospel. A heart of wisdom deals with grief honestly and redemptively. Anything short of that enables grief to fester and cause a sickness of soul.

We Must Be Truthful in Our Grief

There are many temptations to offset or deny the pain of losing an unbelieving loved one. Each temptation offers us a way to lessen the profound anguish, but none of us can afford the price. Our pain stems from the truth: an unbeliever's death causes that person to be separated not only from us but also from God . . . forever. Temptations to ease that pain involve deviation from the truth. We do not want to be dishonest; we are simply trying not to hurt so much. If we allow ourselves to become desperate for relief from grief, we may loosen our grip on truth.

We may be tempted to create an illusion. Many people seek to manage their pain over the death of an unbeliever by saying, "Who knows, what if at the last moment, just before she passed into eternity, she said yes to Y'shua?" The more they dwell on this, the more certain they become that it is precisely what happened.

There are even those who insist that God personally revealed to them that beloved relatives had been saved, even though the relatives never indicated that they wanted Y'shua. Certainly God can reveal whatever He wants to whomever He chooses. But God does not reveal to anyone anything that is contrary to His Word or contrary to reality. I believe in the possibility of "death-bed conversions" viz-à-viz the thief on the cross. Yet even the thief on the cross *confessed his faith.*

We must never discount the grace of God, yet we cannot trade the truth for a pain remedy. People who insist that loved ones were saved at the last moment without any kind of evidence may not realize that they have violated their loved one's right to choose. They also show a lack of trust in God. Creating illusions regarding unbelieving loved ones trivializes reality. Like all illusions, it may look like a blanket in cold weather, but the person who trusts in it for warmth could freeze to death.

We may be tempted into denial. A Jewish believer who has lost unbelieving loved ones can seek to ease the pain by thinking that heaven and hell are not that important. Perhaps the reality of the afterlife dims. Then the reality of Christ and His cross become diminished in that person's eyes. What was once held to be true is no longer accepted, not because it is any less true but because of the pain we feel over those who perish without that truth. In order to avoid that pain, some are tempted to avoid the Bible, praying and fellowship: in short, they are tempted to avoid all those things that point to the painful truth.

When the truth hurts, it is natural to avoid it. What we need to realize is that the truth doesn't change if we stop believing it. Any relief we might feel from avoiding the truth comes at our own peril. There is a time to mourn and a time to grieve; there is a time to weep and a time to wail. The death of a loved one outside of Christ causes pain that we cannot soften or avoid if we want to function within reality.

We may be tempted to create a different, nonbiblical theology in order to ease our pain. Some allow themselves to believe that people are saved by sincerity and good intentions. They are convinced that if their loved one had known that Jesus was the Lord, he or she would have believed, and that God somehow reckons this as faith. This kind of theological shape shifting trivializes the cross and makes what the Messiah did for us into a cruel joke. If

God accepts people based on what they would have chosen rather than on what they actually chose, Jesus should not have had to die at all. When brought to its logical conclusion, it implies that Y'shua's suffering in the Garden of Gethsemane should have been enough since God knew that He was sincere and willing to make the supreme sacrifice. That kind of thinking is contrary to Scripture. We were not saved through Y'shua's sincerity, but rather through His atoning death and resurrection. We must not succumb to the temptation to bend the truth for the sake of lessening our grief.

We may be tempted by the notion of a second chance. It would be comforting to believe that there is some cosmic way station after death. We know God is merciful, so why not believe that He will give another chance to people who had what we feel are hindrances to faith? It would be comforting to believe this, but there is no biblical basis for the idea. In fact, the Bible indicates just the opposite, "And as it is appointed for men to die once, but after this the judgment, so Christ was offered once to bear the sins of many. To those who eagerly wait for Him He will appear a second time, apart from sin, for salvation" (Hebrews 9:27-28). As surely as Jesus is coming again, so judgment comes after death. We cannot argue for grace beyond what Scripture allows.

How can we avoid the temptation to be less than honest when we grieve over unbelieving loved ones? In the end we must trust all of our loved ones to God. The one thing that enables us to survive the death of unsaved loved ones is the knowledge that God is just and loving. God does all things well; we cannot understand but we can trust Him. One day we will know as we are known. We must know now that what we will know then will satisfy all the questions of the heart.

Meanwhile, grief for those who don't believe must move us to pray, to witness ever more boldly, to risk everything so that while they are yet living, they may hear and be saved. And we must not deny our pain when those who were not saved die.

A heart of wisdom bears the pain of death as part of life's reality. We come to the Lord with our pain and tell Him we hurt. He does not remove the pain any more than He removes the reality, but He lets us know that we are not alone, and we are able to bear real grief with Him as our comforter.

Part of our comfort is that we can count on His promise: that a day will come when there shall be no crying or mourning—the day when every tear shall be dried and His presence will fill our hearts with understanding and joy.

How Do We Interact With Others as We Grieve?

If a family member has died and your relatives are sitting *shiva,* no matter what it takes for you to be there, it is good to spend all seven days in mourning. This enables you to enter into the family grief and also to be a witness to the living.

Part of the reason for grief is to release the departed person. That is why we need the funeral and why sitting *shiva* helps. People spend time with one another missing the person who died and accepting the fact that there is a profound absence. Mirrors are covered so the mourners need not be reminded of their grief-altered appearance and are not tempted to vanity. A *minyon*[5] gathers for prayer so the mourners need not leave the house for worship.

This is a time when people are thinking about life and death so there is a chance for discussion and an opportunity to tell of your hope in the Messiah. It can be a good time for witnessing, but it is not a time to hand out tracts. Ask God for wisdom to offer a word of life and hope in a way that the mourners will receive. If you are the only believing member of your family, you may be excluded from participating in certain parts of the funeral. Don't let that keep you from attending.

I was in Israel with a group of Jewish Christian college students when our teacher/guide Dr. Fruchtenbaum received a phone call from his wife, MaryAnn. His father had passed away, and the funeral was set to take place in fewer than 48 hours.

I know that Dr. Fruchtenbaum really struggled over what he should do. His family had planned the funeral without him and had left little time for him to return. It would have been easy for

---

5. *Minyon:* a quorum of ten males past the age of 13 that is required for Jewish public worship.

him to be offended by the slight and to reason that he had a responsibility to the tour. Instead, he made the arduous journey to Los Angeles, arriving just in time for the funeral. I believe Dr. Fruchtenbaum made the right decision. He reported upon his return to Israel that he had been asked to say *Kaddish*[6] on behalf of the entire family. God honors our efforts to do what is right.

How do you eulogize a loved one who didn't believe? You need to speak of the things that you appreciated about the person, but you also want the opportunity to share the hope people can have in Y'shua. You can stand up and say, "First of all, I need to tell you where my father and I had some differences." Then you can tell briefly and concisely what Y'shua means to you. For a transition you might say something such as, "Dad never pretended to support my faith, but where some fathers might have turned their backs on their children, he respected my right to think for myself and arrive at my own conclusions." Then go on to tell of his other attributes. In other cases it may be appropriate to say, "If so and so were able to speak today, I believe he/she would want you to know about the reality of life after death." Then speak of God's salvation in Messiah.

What about relating to the bereaved in general, not merely our own family? Unfortunately, comfort is an art that has practically been lost, except for the act of choosing a greeting card. James 1:27 tells us, "Pure and undefiled religion before God and the Father is this: to visit orphans and widows in their trouble." We demonstrate our love for God by consoling those who grieve. Death is a wound to the living, and we must be willing to dress and wrap that wound for them.

We can comfort the survivors; we can pray for them; we can pray for family members to manage their grief well. During *shiva* we can visit and read Psalms out loud to those who care to hear. We can send condolence cards to all who need them. We can mourn with those who are mourning. Too many of us have so protected ourselves from pain that we have lost our ability to cry. If we ask God, He will give us the ability to weep with those

---

6. *Kaddish:* a prayer in praise of God recited at certain points in Jewish worship services and specifically at other times in memory of the dead.

who need to weep. Y'shua wept at the tomb of his friend Lazarus. He entered into the grief of Mary and Martha, and so should we enter into the grief of those people whom God has placed in our lives.

When we help someone in his or her grief, we must not seek to diminish that reality with platitudes or say what the grieving person knows to be true. Most often it is not what we say but what we do that makes a difference. Job's comforters started out well. They wept when they saw Job. They sat on the ground without saying a word for seven days and seven nights. If they had stopped there, they would have done well. But they ceased to minister when they began to speak and to seek explanations.

A heart of wisdom responds to grief in simple and sensitive ways: through an invitation to dinner, by including in a family outing a child who has lost his father. Acts of kindness provide comfort and can go beyond comfort to encourage healing.

Facing the Death of a Believer

We face the death of a believing loved one with mixed feelings. We grieve, knowing we will live the rest of life on earth without that person. It could be a loss that requires you to figure out how to go on as a single parent. It might mean finding a way to live without the advice of a cherished mentor or the security of a loving parent. There is no denying the pain. Yet there is, or should be, a sense of rejoicing to know that they are in the presence of the Lord. Not only are these loved ones enjoying Him forever, but we will see them again!

It is important to allow ourselves to have those mixed feelings. If we deny that it is painful to go on without a believing loved one, we carry that pain alone. There is nothing unspiritual about allowing ourselves to feel a terrible sense of loss.

It is important to be honest with ourselves about the loss so that others can help us bear our burden, and we can adjust our lives to function without that person. But it is also important to keep our loss in perspective. It is a temporary loss felt in a world that is quickly passing away. The joy we will have at our union with the Messiah and reunion of loved ones in Him should never be too far from our thoughts.

When a believing loved one dies you can establish a memorial gift that shows the meaning of that person's life. At the Jews for Jesus training center in New York City we have the Rachmiel Frydland Memorial Chapel. Those who knew Rachmiel know of his untiring commitment to telling our Jewish people about Y'shua. It is fitting, then, to have such a place in his honor where Jewish people can hear the Good News. It is wonderful to have lasting tributes to those whom we love in the Lord.

How Do We Prepare for Our Own Death?

Some of the mishpochah have asked about what is involved in having a Jewish funeral and burial. Many of us already have burial plots purchased for us by our families. Certain problems may arise from this. If you own cemetery property, it is probably illegal for anyone to keep you from being buried there. Yet I know of cases where this was done to Jewish believers because of their faith.

It would be wonderful if there were provision for messianic cemeteries. The American Board of Missions to the Jews, now Chosen People Ministries, at one time purchased a section of a cemetery in New York for Jewish believers. For most of us, this isn't an option. Therefore, we have to ask, is it good to be buried in a Jewish cemetery by a rabbi? Definitely not!

If an unbelieving rabbi performs your funeral, some might say that you renounced Jesus and "went back to Judaism" before you died. Your funeral might very well be used as proof that you turned from Christ at the last moment. Even if that is not the case, you won't have the gospel preached at your service. The message of one who does not share your hope will be the last official words spoken on your behalf.

Most of us wouldn't think of moving from one city to the next without filling out change of address forms, letting family and friends know where we will be. In a sense, when God calls us home to be with Him, we need to fill out one final change of address form. That is the best way for us to make sure that those we leave behind can find us and join us in our new home. If there is ever a time when we ought to be a testimony, it is upon our death. The funeral can serve that purpose.

I think it is very important to have a will that includes your wishes concerning the details of your own funeral. Planning it yourself is the only way to be certain you will get what you want. You can pick the songs that you want sung. You can even make a cassette to greet people who come to your funeral. You can decide now what you will tell them.

For example, a believer's message might be:

Shalom! Thank you for coming to honor my memory. I want to let you know that I'm not just a memory because I've invested my life with Y'shua HaMashiach. I'm not in the body that is going in the ground. I am in the presence of the Lord, and I can truly say that I am happier than I have ever been! I know this by faith, and you can know it too. If you put your trust in Jesus, you will enter into that joy. You will have a bit of heaven inside of you while you walk this earth, and you won't have to be afraid of death. Okay, now I especially want to tell my brother . . .

Then you can greet different ones in the family and tell them how you have appreciated them. You might even conclude by saying:

This is the last time you will hear from me unless you invest your life in Y'shua. I hope you will because if you do, I know that soon we are going to have a joyous reunion in a much better place.

The most important thing about our funeral is not *where* we are buried but *how* we are buried. If you decide to make it so, what takes place at your funeral can be a testimony to unsaved family and friends that Jesus is alive and so are you.

Near the end of his life, D. L. Moody said, "Soon you will read in the newspapers that Moody is dead. Don't you believe it, for I shall be more alive than I am now." That is our hope and our testimony.

Some of us have gotten well past the fear of death, but we still fear the actual process of dying. We can ask the Lord to help us die well, not knowing what the circumstances will be, but desiring to glorify Him in all things.

And though we might tremble a bit in thinking of walking through that door, we need not fear. For we will surely awaken, not as dreamers from a nightmare, but as beloved citizens of our true home, radiant as we greet our Heavenly Host.

"But God will redeem my soul from the power of the grave, for He shall receive me" (Psalm 49:15).

Part Four

Walking Through (Not Around) Tough Issues

Symbols and Substance

A twentieth-century religious movement known as the Cargo Cults threatened to destroy many tribal peoples. These Cargo Cults were particularly destructive in Melanesia, where local people observed how missionaries and colonial officials received supplies that dropped as cargo from the skies or came in from the ocean. They regarded these "gifts" from the context of their own religious beliefs, imitated a foreign culture and expected the skies and oceans to yield cargo to them as well. They adopted such practices and outward behavior as eating their meals at tables and sitting on chairs rather than squatting—because it seemed necessary to please whatever gods had sent the cargo. People abandoned their agrarian lifestyle. Gardening ceased; livestock and crops were neglected *as people devoted their time and energy to building symbolic airstrips, docks and warehouses to receive and store cargo that never came.* You can imagine the disastrous results.

How could people get themselves into such a predicament? Some might say it was because they were unsophisticated, primitive or naive. Those things may or may not be true, but they wouldn't account for such a drastic change in lifestyle. I think the problem was that these people did not know how to do something that had never before been necessary in their culture. They endangered their families and their communities because they had a mistaken notion of cause and effect. **They did not know how to distinguish between symbol and substance.**

Failure to distinguish between symbol and substance is not found exclusively in unsophisticated societies. If it were, we would not have expressions such as "clothes make the man." Some people go into debt to own a particular car in hopes of receiving the treatment they believe naturally accrues to people who drive such cars. Many couples spend incredible amounts of time and money on their weddings and receptions while investing comparatively little time and effort on developing skills necessary to build the actual marriages.

Failure to distinguish between symbol and substance is

common. It is likely to happen when we want something and begin moving to get what we want before we have thought deeply about it. It is when we fail to think deeply that we are most likely to mistake symbols for substance.

By thinking deeply, I mean asking the kind of questions that will get us down to sources. We need to be analytical to get beyond the surface level. When we want something, we must be careful that we truly understand what we want, why we want it, whether we ought to have it, whether or not it's possible to have it, and if so, *we've got to know the right way to get it.* When we begin to think deeply about those things that we want, we are dealing with matters of substance.

As Jewish believers in Jesus, much of what we value as substantial (faith, heritage and "connectedness" with others who share that faith and heritage) is not apprehended with our five senses. When we look for ways to express or represent matters of spiritual or cultural substance, we utilize symbols. Symbols do not bring substance into being. When properly used, they *represent* substance that already exists. A symbol cannot precede what it represents.

As unique traditions and forms of worship are developed, Jewish believers need to learn to distinguish symbol from substance. Unlike the tribal people of Melanesia, we Jewish believers are not adopting a foreign culture and customs. We are looking for ways to express our own heritage. But unless we think analytically, we risk embracing symbols without substance. The result is a life based on half-truths and illusions. Worse yet, we could embrace a symbol that may even express a substance inimical to our faith in Y'shua. There are substantial theological and cultural prejudices against which we need to guard our hearts.

I believe the following excerpts from letters I've received symbolize the dangers of these two prejudices:

One Jewish believer wrote :

> When you reinterpret Jesus from the Jewish perspective, everything changes, including definitions of salvation, Messiah, God, Son of God, Word of God, Torah, etc. The result, I believe, magnifies rather than diminishes the

importance of Jesus. It also renders him fully acceptable, even potentially important, to *halakhic*[1] Judaism.

Later in his letter he commented:

> The test of a Jew, however, is not doctrine or the strength of their belief, but loyalty—to the uni-un (not triune) God, to their fellow Jews, to Judaism, to Torah and to the Covenant. It is assumed that no matter how secular a Jew becomes, or how far their doctrine strays, they will close ranks and stand with their people should the situation call for it.

> The loyalty of Messianic Jews is open to question because the biggest threat to Judaism historically has come from Christians and because most evangelized Jews end up members of Gentile churches, many of which preach that Judaism is either dead or a pointless anachronism.

> My question is this: The next time Christians start killing Jews in the name of Jesus, will you stand with your people? I have no doubt that you, personally, will. Most Jews, however, have grave doubts about whether their Messianic brothers and sisters can be counted on.

This brother is juggling a number of important issues, and it seems to me that he is unintentionally reducing doctrine (which I believe is a matter of substance) to a symbol—a symbol of Jewish identity. He seems to be saying what you believe (or perhaps refuse to believe) shows your loyalty to the Jewish people. He also seems to say that loyalty is more important than belief or doctrine when it comes to Jewish identity. Identity and loyalty are good and valuable, but it is destructive to elevate them above the substance of doctrine, which is what we believe and teach about God.

Loyalty to the God who created the Jews certainly precedes (but does not preclude) our loyalty to the Jewish people. In the letter, the issue of loyalty is initially listed in the context of loy-

---

1. *Halakhic:* pertaining to the accepted Jewish law or to the way or method of procedure based on the teachings of the Talmud.

alty to God. The writer implies that belief in God's tri-unity is a symbol of disloyalty, an implication that I must categorically deny. But the letter then introduces the theme of loyalty to people, specifically people whose acceptance most Jewish believers would value. This person would have me believe that certain doctrines (i.e., that Jesus is the only way of salvation and that rejecting Him results in an eternity apart from God) symbolizes disloyalty toward unbelieving Jewish people. He believes these doctrines sprang from anti-Jewish sentiments. He contends that if we believe these doctrines, we seem to be against our own people. He seems to say that unbelieving Jews are justified in wondering if we would care about their welfare in times of trouble. At least, that is how I understand his letter.

Loyalty is important. I trust that all of us will continue to identify with our Jewish people, even if we must endure persecution—even death—at the hands of anti-Semites. I also trust that all of us will continue to identify with our Messiah, even when *that* means enduring persecution, and, should the day come, death.

However, doctrine is *not* an expression of loyalty. It is to be believed or not believed, accepted or rejected on one criteria: whether or not it is true. Conversely, the object of genuine loyalty is a person or persons, not a belief. Belief is not always a matter of choice—for an honest person cannot disbelieve that which becomes obvious—but it is always a matter of commitment. If we commit ourselves to believing or not believing in order to get along with others, we are not loyal to them; we are merely unwilling to risk their disapproval. More important, if we choose to believe or disbelieve for the sake of gaining approval, we are not honest with ourselves or God.

Disapproval is a substantial matter. It keeps us from associating with people we love. But to shift our beliefs in order to associate and gain approval demonstrates *dis*loyalty to God. Most people honestly believe they are above such disloyalty. They have many reasons to show that they are doing the right thing rather than the convenient thing.

We need to recognize that basic beliefs about Y'shua and His nature are substance. Symbols are representational and negotiable. Substance is neither. Danger number one is negotiating the non-negotiable nature of Jesus. Danger number two is also apparent in the letter from which I quoted, but is even better illustrated in another letter from a different Jewish believer who is the leader of a ministry. He wrote:

> What we know as Christianity started from the beginning as Pauline synagogues of Gentiles worshiping the Jewish Messiah. Then this group of Gentile believers, lacking the courage to stand up for Y'shua and His religion against persecution, made up their own anti-Jewish religion called Christianity.

In another letter, he went on to say:

> Most of what we see as Christianity, today and historically, is so far from the religion of Y'shua, so pagan and foreign to God's will, so anti-biblical and anti-Jewish, that we have no choice but to view it publicly as an aberration.

This statement is astounding. **Certainly, it only represents a minority of Jewish believers**, but it's frightening to think that anyone in the mishpochah believes such things. This brother is a caring, considerate and sensitive person. Yet the ideas and generalizations he expressed are, in some ways, as inflammatory and prejudicial as the anti-Semitism to which he is reacting. Thus the second danger to our movement is that in attempting to rediscover the Jewishness of our faith, some of our messianic mishpochah might be adopting cultural prejudices.

For *some* of our unbelieving brothers and sisters, finding fault with Gentiles is a symbol of Jewish loyalty. "The enemy of my enemy is my friend." (Just as some anti-Semites consider their hatred of Jews a symbol of loyalty to their own culture or religion.) But true loyalty to one's own is not best expressed through prejudice toward outsiders. Some symbols are poor symbols because they do not accurately represent the substance. Prejudice is a poor symbol. It is a shortcut to expressing affiliation with one group by excluding another.

Prejudice is altogether inimical to our faith in Y'shua who called for unity among believers. Further, anyone who dares to regard most Christians as pagans (and I hope most don't dare) is claiming knowledge of millions of people he has never met and hundreds of thousands of churches he has never visited. I don't think we should tolerate a spirit of Gentile-bashing in ourselves, and I hope that we will gently but firmly let others know it is un-Y'shua-like.

On the other hand, there is much to be said for the desire to express our faith in Jesus within the context of our Jewish identity. For although a minority of Christians still insist that faith in Jesus means repudiating all things Jewish (and the majority of Jews insist the same thing!), we are guided by a very Jewish Jesus. We will not be robbed of our identity by anyone—Jews or non-Jews! As a movement of Jewish Christians, messianic Jews or any other name (symbol) by which we care to be known, we must maintain the integrity of our faith and our heritage. We must be more concerned with substance than symbols.

When considering models and forms of worship to express our faith in a Jewish context, we want to incorporate appropriate Jewish traditions. In order to know what is appropriate, we need to think deeply about what we want. We need to ask ourselves difficult questions to discover if the substance of what we seek is from God. If we don't think deeply, we risk the temptation of shortcuts, i.e. inappropriate symbols. Inappropriate symbols either have no substance behind them or they represent a substance destructive to messianic faith. Compromised doctrine and prejudices that unfairly label or shut out Gentile members of the body of Messiah are destructive to our faith.

How should we guard against these dangers? By carefully analyzing the substance of our faith and our Jewish identity and holding ourselves and others accountable to maintain the integrity of that which is substantial.

One way is by institutionalizing certain symbols that represent the substance of our faith. For example, the doctrinal statement of the Union of Messianic Jewish Congregations includes the declaration:

> We believe in the deity of the Lord Yeshua, the Messiah, in
> His virgin birth, in His sinless life, in His miracles, in His

vicarious and atoning death through His shed blood, in His bodily resurrection, in His ascension to the right hand of the Father, and in His personal return in power and glory.

Various congregations and evangelistic agencies around the world use documents to symbolize their commitment to basic doctrine regarding the nature of Y'shua. Most of these are adaptations of the Nicene Creed.

The Nicene Creed is a doctrinal statement issued by leaders at a church council held in Nicaea in A.D. 325. These church leaders were trying to deal with the false teaching of a man named Arias who denied the deity of Jesus, claiming that He was a created being. In order to deal with this, church leaders put forth a creed that has been accepted throughout the centuries as a true, Scripture-based statement regarding the nature of the Messiah:

> We believe in one God the Father All-sovereign, maker of all things visible and invisible; And in one Lord Jesus Christ, the Son of God, begotten of the Father, only-begotten, that is, of the substance of the Father, God of God, Light of Light, true God of true God, begotten not made, of one substance with the Father, through whom all things were made . . .[2]

I will not go into a lengthy description of the Nicene Creed. For the purpose of this chapter, it is enough to point out that the New Testament clearly teaches the deity of Y'shua. The leadership of the church confirmed that understanding at the Council of Nicaea and put to rest any questions that may have been raised by false teachers such as Arias.

Some Jewish believers have expressed reservations regarding this creed. Some want to reformulate statements such as the Nicene Creed simply to make it more understandable and relevant to Jewish believers. They have no problem with the substance. Dr. John Fischer, chairman of the Theology Committee of the Union of Messianic Jewish Congregations, explains it this way: "We are in agreement on the data. The data will lead you

---

2. Henry Bettenson, ed., *Documents of the Christian Church* (Oxford University Press, 1975), p. 25.

to the conclusion of the Trinity. That's not an issue. The issue is how can we communicate that sensitively, accurately and perhaps in a context that would be a little closer to the original cultural context?"

Dr. Louis Goldberg, retired chairman of the Jewish studies department at Moody Bible Institute and Jews for Jesus scholar-in-residence, adds, "Biblical content stays the same. It is the dress or how you want to talk about it that changes."

People who desire changes that reflect context, not content, are talking about symbols. We "contextualize" so that the language (a symbol) represents doctrines (substance) in a way that is culturally relevant. As we contextualize, we exercise care that the change in symbols/language does not change or misrepresent the substance/doctrines.

Yet there are others who want to alter or dispose of the creeds because they reject the content, that is, the substance of the doctrine. There is a growing minority of Jewish believers who are uncomfortable about openly declaring that Y'shua is God.

One person who questions the Nicene Creed went on to say that he does not agree that Y'shua is co-equal with El Shaddai, the God of the Hebrew Scriptures. Yet the Jesus he describes is not the Jesus of the New Testament. Some people who claim to represent Jewish believers, even on radio and television, have turned to a different Jesus.

In his book *The Jewish Reclamation of Jesus* Donald A. Hagner points out what he calls "some extraordinarily important developments" with regard to Jewish re-examination of the person of Jesus.[3] Likewise, Arthur W. Kac in his book *The Messiahship of Jesus* has cataloged numerous quotes from prominent Jewish personalities that speak highly of the person of Jesus.[4] Many Jewish believers feel greatly encouraged by the statements of people such as Albert Einstein, who declared: "I am a Jew, but I am enthralled by the luminous figure of the

---

3. Donald A. Hagner, *The Jewish Reclamation of Jesus: An Analysis & Critique of the Modern Jewish Study of Jesus* (Grand Rapids, MI: Academie Books, 1984).

4. Arthur W. Kac, *The Messiahship of Jesus: What Jews and Jewish Christians Say* (Chicago: Moody Press, 1980).

Nazarene. . . . No one can read the Gospels without feeling the actual presence of Jesus. His personality pulsates in every word. No myth is filled with such life."[5]

As Jewish believers we, more than any, have a stake in helping the "reclamation" process along. Naturally we would love for our people to accept the Jewishness of Jesus and our own Jewishness as His followers. But in our desire to hasten this, we dare not let ourselves rejoice over statements that seem to be "pro-Y'shua" if they deny His deity. When spokespersons in the Jewish community are sympathetic to their own idea of who Y'shua is, we might feel that represents or symbolizes approval of our faith. But what is the substance of our faith? Either Y'shua is Lord of all or not Lord at all.

The Jewish believer quoted as suggesting that Y'shua "could be fully acceptable and potentially important to *halakhic* Judaism" wrote to me stating,

> Rebbe Zalman Schacter, founder of the Jewish Renewal movement, has stated that he would have no problem accepting a Nazarene Hasidic movement, provided it remained "inside the loop" of *halakhic* Judaism and submitted to *halakhic* authority.

This is precisely the argument that brings us back to the controversy of the first century. Y'shua was unwilling to submit to halakhic authority—which is no more or less than the interpretation of certain rabbis—because He Himself is the author of life—and of the Scriptures. How could Y'shua yield His substantial authority to the ascribed (hence symbolic) authority of these rabbis? No doubt He found many of their interpretations good and correct. But because Jesus *is* God, *halakhah*[6] must submit to His authority and not vice versa.

It is significant that well-known author Rabbi Jacob Neusner has recognized much of the substance of our faith in his book *A Rabbi Talks With Jesus: An Intermillennial, Interfaith Exchange.* He declares:

---

5. *Saturday Evening Post* (October 26, 1929).
6. *Halakhah:* the body of teaching in the Talmud that interprets Jewish law.

No one can encounter Matthew's Jesus without concurring that before us in the evangelist's mind is God incarnate. . . . Several generations of Jewish apologists have fulsomely praised this "Galilean miracle worker," placing him in the tradition of Elijah and the Hasidic rabbis of the eighteenth century and afterward. Other generations have praised Jesus as a great rabbi. These evasions of the Christian claim to truth will serve no more. Christianity does not believe in the Galilean miracle worker, nor does Christianity worship a rabbi. For my part, I will not evade. I will not concede. I will not praise with excessive, irrelevant compliments someone else's God. . . . If not Messiah, God incarnate, then to what grand issue of faith does my affirmation of a rabbi's or prophet's teaching pertain? These concessions express a disingenuous evasion of the issue. They mask a more sincere denial.[7]

Neusner, of course, is not a believer in Jesus and would undermine our faith if he could—in fact, this book attempts to do so. Nevertheless, Neusner demonstrates that the New Testament clearly shows Jesus as God Incarnate.

Yet some believers fail to recognize what an unbeliever such as Neusner sees so clearly. They have a fuzzy idea of what the New Testament teaches and thus they risk compromising the substance of our faith. Efforts to recast Y'shua in a mold more palatable to the Jewish community may be well-intended. Yet if any such attempts compromise the content of our historic faith, they introduce false teaching into the body of Messiah. The effects will be just as deadly as if the intent had been evil.

No'am Hendren, one of our messianic brothers in Israel, succinctly expresses this concern.

In the praiseworthy attempts of messianic Jewish teachers to find forms of expression which will communicate to our people without culturally insensitive "noise," there will always be the temptation to use the theological agenda and

---

7. Jacob Neusner, *A Rabbi Talks With Jesus: An Intermillennial, Interfaith Exchange* (New York: Doubleday, 1993), pp. 15, 16.

terminology of traditional Judaism: an agenda and terminology forged in the heat of controversy with the Church which will not accommodate a divine Messiah.[8]

Let's not lose sight of substance in the quest for symbols, that is, the contemporary Jewish terminology.

As for fighting the danger of anti-Gentile prejudice, it is certainly understandable that some respond to anti-Jewish behavior by forming their own prejudice against non-Jews. The term *goyishe kopf* [9] is not a compliment. A cultural prejudice that many of our Jewish people succumb to is one of making sweeping generalizations about Gentiles. For many, Billy Graham, Adolph Hitler and the Pope all fall into the same category. We cannot make that mistake in the messianic community. To do so would be terribly detrimental to the messianic Jewish movement, because it cuts us off from much of the rest of the body of Messiah.

We need to carefully sort out right and wrong, good and bad. If prejudice has been a part of our cultural identity, then it is one part we need to leave at Calvary. We were raised to a new life with Y'shua. When we were reborn, we did not begin our new life as Gentiles! But neither were we reborn to relearn prejudice as a method of defense. We don't need protective walls of prejudice when Y'shua is our Rock! And since Y'shua died for Jews and Gentiles, we need to regard both as very precious in His sight.

How can we claim our right to express our faith in Jesus within our own Jewish culture, and then deny Gentiles the right to express that faith in their own culture? Commenting on this, Dr. Goldberg observes, "Anti-Gentilism is as bad as anti-Semitism. I have no problem if Gentile believers want to contextualize biblical truth."

Moishe Rosen, founder of Jews for Jesus, gave an address to a meeting of the Lausanne Consultation on Jewish Evangelism

---

8. No'am Hendren, "Response to paper by Walter Riggans: 'The Christological Question and Contemporary Messianic Jewish Movements,'" *Lausanne Consultation on Jewish Evangelism Fourth International Conference Zeist,* Holland 1991, (August 7), p. 152.

9. *Goyishe kopf:* literally "Gentile head"; one who thinks in an un-Jewish way.

titled, "My Challenge to the Churches." He spoke of four different churches: the counterfeit church, the carnal church, the confused church and the committed church. What shall we say about the committed church, the body of Messiah that is truly seeking to please the Lord? We must be prepared to say as Moishe did in his address, "Thank you. Thank you for showing me Y'shua."

He went on to say, "Perhaps one of the greatest stains on the honor of the messianic movement is the way we sometimes have been unjustifiably harsh in our criticism of the churches!"[10]

God had to deal with our brother, the Apostle Peter, concerning his anti-Gentile attitude. Most are familiar with Peter's vision in Acts 10:10-15. It took Peter three visions to get the point, and the point wasn't about eating *trayf.*[11] God was preparing Peter to go to the house of Cornelius, a Gentile, to proclaim the gospel to him.

Perhaps some of us need to hear the voice of the Lord saying, "What God has cleansed, we no longer can consider unholy." We need to embrace our brothers and sisters in the Lord who may have different cultural expressions, whose ancestors may have persecuted ours, but who now have been joined to us through the perfect bond of peace, Y'shua our Messiah.

As we Jewish believers desire to recover the Jewishness of our faith, we need to think deeply so that we may achieve our goal through discernment and humility, not mistaking symbol for substance. Let's be quick to reject those theological and cultural prejudices that darken the hearts and minds of our people to the truth of the gospel. As we claim our heritage, let's go for the substance and embrace the symbols that allow us to hold fast to what is good. Let's do so as the righteous remnant, faithful to our heritage, faithful to our family in the body of Christ and most of all, faithful to the Messiah, Jesus.

---

10. Moishe Rosen, "My Challenge to the Churches," *Lausanne Consultation on Jewish Evangelism Fourth International Conference Zeist,* Holland 1991, (August 8-9), p. 218.

11. *Trayf:* unclean according to Jewish dietary laws, i.e. pork, shellfish, etc. that are forbidden in Leviticus 11; the term also refers to clean animals not slaughtered in the prescribed rabbinic way.

Wonder of Wonders! Miracle of Miracles!

The door burst open and in rushed the *shammes*,[1] his eyes alight with holy fervor. "Rabbi!" he shouted, upon entering the *tzaddik's*[2] study. "A cripple just approached the *bimah*,[3] laid his hand on the Torah and threw his crutches away! I witnessed the whole thing!"

The rabbi, a Hassid known throughout Lithuania as a wonder worker, jumped up from his chair and raised his hands heavenward. "A miracle from heaven!" he cried, his face aglow with spiritual rapture. "But where is the man now?"

"Lying in the aisle," answered the *shammes*. "The poor man fell on his *tuchus*!"[4]

If jokes are supposed to lighten our hearts in the midst of tragedy, it is no wonder that the subject of miracles has its place in *The Encyclopedia of Jewish Humor.* Considering our heritage and the many miracles God performed for our ancestors, it is indeed tragic that many view those miracles as no more than myths, legends or ancient evidence of a God who once cared for us but hasn't done much to prove it lately. Those who do not know God may try to ease their pain by laughing at their own unfulfilled expectations, but the joke raises a serious question for us who know the Lord: do we really believe in miracles?

Do We Believe in Miracles?

Many find it difficult to accept the possibility of the miraculous while others are convinced that we should always "expect a miracle." Our own experiences can mislead us either way.

Skeptics may attempt to guard themselves or others from disappointment or deception. Perhaps they have experienced such

---

1. *Shammes:* a servant; caretaker or sexton of a synagogue who distributes prayer books and prayer shawls to the worshipers and who may perform various religious duties in the absence of a cantor or officiant.

2. *Tzaddik:* a righteous person.

3. *Bimah:* the synagogue platform from where the Scriptures are read.

4. *Tuchus:* posterior anatomy upon which one normally sits.

Condensed from Henry D. Spaulding, ed., *The Encyclopedia of Jewish Humor* (New York: Jonathan David Publishers, 1969), p. 81.

disappointment or deception in the past.

Have you ever asked God to perform a miracle, such as healing a terminally ill family member or friend? Was that person healed? If not, perhaps you are skeptical of miracles because you once had hope that led to disappointment and despair. This is understandable. Yet we must be careful, lest such skepticism cause us to doubt God and rob us of the joy of knowing He is at work in our lives.

On the other hand, our experiences can produce emotions that cause us to see "miracle-mirages;" that is, to think we see a miracle where in fact there is none. Remember Mottel the Tailor in "Fiddler on the Roof?" Upon his engagement to Tseitel, Tevya's oldest daughter, Mottel runs through the woods exclaiming, "Wonder of wonders! Miracle of miracles!" He recounts many of the miracles of our Jewish people in times past: our deliverance from Egypt, the collapsed walls of Jericho, the slaying of Goliath. But to Mottel the Tailor, the most miraculous one of all is that God made him a man and is giving him a bride in Tseitel.

For Mottel the Tailor the "miracle" was an improbable wish that had come true. The match required no divine display, no suspension of the laws of nature, yet for Mottel it provided a reminder that God cared enough to bring unexpected blessing. In his euphoria, receiving his heart's desire seemed like a miracle. Or perhaps Mottel felt that in his impoverished state and homely appearance, becoming engaged to Tseitel truly was a miracle! Maybe you have received some unexpected blessing in which God's grace is so plain that you cannot help but feel it is a miracle.

Whether we accept the miraculous may be influenced to a large extent by our own experience or lack thereof. But our committed belief in the reality of the living God (or lack thereof) can also play a deciding role in how we view miracles.

In discussing this issue, we also need to realize that the word *miracle* may mean different things to different people. It isn't possible to be comprehensive in defining supernatural events, but for the sake of clarity we can describe some of the things we do and don't mean when referring to miracles.

What Is a Miracle?

Our Jewish tradition paints a picture of the miraculous in broad strokes. Rabbis have taught that the regular order of daily life is a miracle. This is clearly stated in our *siddur*.[5] In the *Amidah*[6] for the daily prayer service we read, "For your miracles that are with us every day; and for your wonders and favors in every season evening, morning and afternoon."[7]

The idea that all of life can be considered one gigantic miracle that God is continuously performing is beautiful and right inasmuch as nothing would exist without God. Yet it is imprecise to label all of life a miracle and to do so raises confusion about the meaning of specific miraculous events. Why speak of the miracles in Egypt or at Mount Carmel or even the miracles Y'shua performed, if the rising of the sun each day is just as much a miracle?

God *is* involved in the rising and setting of the sun, the changing seasons, the cycle of birth and, in fact, every aspect of creation. But it is more appropriate to use the word *providence* when discussing the Lord's presence and power that is daily made manifest in His creation and in His dealings with us. Providence is God's continuing care for and involvement with all existing things; it is the provision He makes for us and for the carrying out of His will in this world.

God's providence should be no less a source of wonder and amazement for us than His miracles. And God's care for us goes beyond providence as we see specific answers to prayer. Many people claim that God has performed "small miracles" for them: the highly unlikely parking spot in just the right place, the abnormally quick recovery from the flu, or the ability to quit smoking or drinking without the usual cravings or withdrawal symptoms. We might call these phenomenal answers to prayer. Let me give you an example. This is a testimony of Ilana, a Jewish believer who has known the Lord for fourteen years:

---

5. *siddur:* Jewish prayer book.

6. *Amidah:* literally *standing* is the name of an important prayer to be said standing up.

7. Rabbi Nossin Sherman, ed., *The Complete Art Scroll Siddur* (New York: Mesorah, 1984), p. 113.

I was brought up Reform and kinda lost my way. My sister-in-law was a believer and tried to talk to me about Y'shua. I was headstrong and would not listen.

Due to a mix-up in paperwork the Army, where my husband was employed, deducted $600 from his pay. I didn't work and we needed every penny of his pay. As I walked down the field, I spoke to God as I was known to do. Well, this time I said, "If Jesus is really Your Son—give me back the $600." When I got home, I found a check in the mailbox for exactly the amount of money the Army had taken. It was a settlement from a car wreck I had had seven years before and had forgotten about.

It may be coincidence, but it was enough for me. This turned my life around.

Judas turned in Y'shua for 20 pieces of silver. God "bought" me for $600. It sounds weird and illogical, but by the very sense that it is not logical no one can convince me that Y'shua is not the Messiah.

God told me and I believe it and that's that.

Now that's what I call a phenomenal answer to prayer! Perhaps you have had an experience similar to Ilana's.

These answers to prayer are occasions to praise God. They stand as testimonies to the fact that He hears our petitions. They go beyond providence because they demonstrate in a personal way God's involvement and His loving care in arranging the circumstances of our lives. Yet I would not call even these phenomenal answers to prayer miracles.

Perhaps the simplest definition of a miracle is C. S. Lewis' "an interference with nature by supernatural power."[8]

Lewis indicates that in order for an event to qualify as a miracle, it must be contrary to or beyond the realm of what could possibly naturally occur. The Bible gives us examples of such events: Lot's wife turned to a pillar of salt, manna coming from

---

8. C. S. Lewis, *Miracles* (New York: Macmillan, 1947), p. 5.

heaven on every day but the Sabbath, Elijah's calling down fire from heaven. These events were clearly outside of the natural order. What shall we say of Jesus raising Lazarus from the dead even after his flesh had begun to stink? Jesus' own resurrection to a body that was no longer subject to death's decay is the greatest miracle ever witnessed by any human being.

We who believe the Bible and know that God is real recognize His providence as well as His personal care for us in those occasions whereby, as Corrie ten Boom said, "God raises the level of the impossible." But if we believe in God, we must also be willing to accept that He who created the universe is certainly able to "interrupt" at will the order that He created.

Skepticism or Unbelief?

We should believe in miracles because we believe in God. Some of us also believe in miracles because we have witnessed them. When we speak of such miracles, we must expect to face some skepticism. When it comes to the unsaved, we have to remember that true skeptics have a real question in their mind as to whether they should believe. If they are really questioning, they will be open to God's answer, no matter how He chooses to give it. If they are not true skeptics, they might try to appear objective by raising doubts about God's activity in our lives and by asking questions they think are unanswerable. But there are only real answers for those who have real questions.

Y'shua declared that His miracles were evidence of His deity. Those who witnessed the miracles but rejected His claims, took up stones to stone him. Y'shua said, "I showed you many good works (i.e. miracles) from the father; for which of them are you stoning me?"

Brothers and sisters, things have not changed all that much. Presented with the evidence and answers to their questions, how can today's skeptics respond? They can either accept the evidence or doggedly attempt to explain it away while searching for other questions to ask and other doubts to raise. If they persist in doing the latter, they are no longer an objective skeptic but a committed unbeliever.

What about skepticism in the believer regarding miracles,

particularly miracles today? We walk a fine line here, for we cannot allow skepticism to cast doubt on who God is. His all-powerful sovereignty dictates that miracles must always be a possibility. On the other hand, there is a sense in which skepticism can be healthy.

In preparing to write about miracles, I invited *Mishpochah Message* readers to send in accounts of any miraculous healings that have taken place in their lives. We also asked that independent verification be provided for these healings. We received a number of inspiring testimonies. Yet there was no one who had an instance where a medical test had been made to diagnose a condition with a corresponding test made later to show that a healing took place that was contrary to the laws of nature.

One person on Jews for Jesus' regular mailing list (who does not receive the *Mishpochah Message*) claimed to have a healing where a diagnosis of bone cancer was recorded. She said that tests were done after the alleged healing showing that the cancer had disappeared. In fact, the person explained that the doctor himself had been healed of cancer. When we called to verify this with the doctor whose name had been supplied, he was quite adamant in telling us that he had no idea what we were talking about and that he didn't "hold to that sort of thing." Sadly, this type of experience is all too common.

When a good friend of mine, a Jewish believer who is a medical doctor, heard that we were going to publish an article on miracles, he wrote a word of caution. My friend had done some personal investigation to verify the miracles in a number of books written concerning signs and wonders. He read the books thinking God might be calling him into a healing ministry, but to his dismay he found each of the instances where healing was claimed to be questionable.

My friend knows and loves the Lord and believes that God works in the lives of people today. He believes in the miracles of the Bible and believes that God is the same yesterday, today and forever. His caution was based on his own experience and training as a medical doctor as well as the conclusions he drew from researching various believers' claims to the miraculous.

Don't misunderstand—I am not saying that God does not do

miraculous healing today! But such miracles are not as common as many people would like to believe. Proper questioning of claims to the miraculous is not a sign of unbelief; truth is never threatened by honest questioning. When Jesus healed the lepers, He told them to show themselves to the priests. He expected, even commanded them to verify the miracle.

Miracles: Can We Expect Too Much?

While some people (even believers) miss out on God's blessings because of their unbelief, others emphasize the importance of miracles to a level that is unhealthy for their faith and testimony. Sometimes they are so hungry for the reality of God in their lives that they are willing to call things miracles when they are not.

If we lower the standard of what we consider the miraculous in our lives, we not only tend to delude ourselves, but we can also cast a cloud over the case for the lordship of Y'shua in the eyes of unbelievers.

An overemphasis on miracles usually reflects one of two false teachings: that miracles are sufficient to produce faith or that faith is sufficient to produce miracles.

Some people believe that miracles are the most effective means of convincing unbelievers of the gospel truth.

Have you ever thought that if only God would perform a miracle of great significance for your family, they would have to believe in Y'shua?

After all, John wrote, "And truly Jesus did many other signs in the presence of His disciples, which are not written in this book; but these are written that you may believe that Jesus is the Christ, the Son of God, and that believing you may have life in His name" (John 20:30-31). Does this mean that Jesus' miracles are to reach through time into the heart of the unbelieving reader and produce faith?

Certainly many believed when they saw Y'shua's miracles, but Y'shua himself did not entrust Himself to those who believed in Him because of the signs He performed.

"Now when He was in Jerusalem at the Passover, during the feast, many believed in His name when they saw the signs which

He did. But Jesus did not commit Himself to them, because He knew all men, and had no need that anyone should testify of man, for He knew what was in man" (John 2:23-25). Those who were closest to Y'shua were drawn to Him and followed Him because He was true:

> "Lord, to whom shall we go? You have the words of eternal life. Also we have come to believe and know that You are the Christ, the Son of the living God." (John 6:68, 69)

If we expect people to believe on the basis of a miracle, we will be disappointed. A Jewish believer told the story of her aunt Miriam who was dying of cancer. Doctors said she would not live beyond a few weeks. The believing niece visited Miriam in the hospital. She recounted how the Lord had given her a word of knowledge that her aunt would be healed. Within a few days, the woman had a complete remission. That was fifteen years ago. Miriam is still alive—and still an unbeliever. She felt the "word" was merely coincidental.

What about Ilana's testimony? Does her coming to faith after a phenomenal answer to prayer make her a second-class believer? Not at all! God in His wisdom knew the best way to confront her skepticism, and in His grace He made Himself known in the circumstances of her life. But He also knew that her heart was ready to receive the truth. Another person might have explained the $600 away as coincidence. We spoke to Ilana before including her story. While God used an unusual means of bringing her to faith, since then it has not been the basis for her commitment to the Lord.

Miraculous experiences can be building blocks for faith; they can act to get our attention or to confirm something that we are already willing to believe—but they will never do as the foundation. If experiences are the building blocks, then Scripture is the mortar that holds our faith together.

Ultimately our faith must be based on truth of the *gospel* miracle: that Jesus the Messiah died for our sins and rose from the dead on the third day according to Scripture. We must reject the notion that other miracles, signs and wonders are necessary for effective evangelism. Remember the words of "doubting"

Thomas who declared, "Unless I see in His hands the print of the nails, and put my finger into the print of the nails, and put my hand into His side, I will not believe" (John 20:25). After Thomas recognized the Lord, Y'shua said, "Because you have seen Me, you have believed. Blessed are those who have not seen and yet have believed" (John 20:29). That is still true today.

The only supernatural act required to bring our families to faith is the working of the Holy Spirit to open their eyes, to soften their hearts and to unstop their ears so that they might receive Him. We must pray without ceasing for that miracle.

Equally erroneous is the notion that faith produces miracles. God is not a machine to be operated by our faith. We are seriously mistaken if we think verses such as Matthew 17:20 mean that if we believe hard enough, God will do whatever we wish. Having faith means a joining of our mind and our heart to God's. It means accepting His truth as our reality. *Faith does not give us control. It allows us to accept God's control.* It is not channeling God's power for our purposes. It is believing and submitting to His power for His purposes.

Nor can we insist that we will get our miracle based on the idea that it will glorify God. God will glorify Himself. If we want to glorify Him we can do that every day by obeying Him. I believe that God indeed performs miracles to glorify Himself. But we cannot count on a miracle merely because we have believed hard enough and promised to give Him the glory.

It is all too easy for us to deceive ourselves: to want something so badly that we are convinced that God has promised it to us, to claim it in faith, and then have to deal with the disappointment when we don't get what we thought God promised.

I have a dear friend who, in her grief over the loss of her mom, became angry with God. She doubted her faith and questioned the Savior's love. Her mother—who was a believer in Y'shua—had been ill for several years, so death did not come suddenly. *Yet it came as a surprise to my friend because she had led herself to believe that God would heal her mother.* She had asked God for a sign that He would heal her mother, and she believed God had given her that sign. She was wrong.

I don't want to minimalize the very natural grief and sense of loss my friend went through, nor her real need to feel pain and sorrow over that loss. Yet I can't help but think that she missed out on the hope and joy that she might experience as a believer, knowing that her mother is with the Lord.

The Bible tells us that "this perishable must put on the imperishable, this mortal must put on immortality." For those of us in Christ, death is swallowed up in victory. If we focus too much on healing miracles, we can change the experience of death from a triumphal entry into heaven to a defeat that causes us to leave the field of battle. To live is Christ, but brothers and sisters, to die is such greater gain than any temporary healing could bring. Let's not set ourselves up for such disappointment by expecting miracles God never promised us.

To believe and claim miracles is not wrong. Yet our insistence upon the miraculous can sometimes be a sign of spiritual weakness. Y'shua said, "An evil and adulterous generation seeks after a sign, and no sign will be given to it except the sign of the prophet Jonah" (Matthew 12:39). The religious leaders of Y'shua's day demanded a sign. He refused to accede to their wishes. God does not need to prove anything to anyone. He is the sovereign Lord of creation! And He has already revealed Himself to us by sending His son to die and rise again from the dead. This is the sign of Jonah. We need no further demonstrations of His love and care, though God in His grace and sovereign timing is sometimes pleased to provide them.

Many people talk of "their miracle" as though it somehow elevates their spiritual status, shows how important they really are. A hunger for the miraculous is *sometimes* an indictment of our faithlessness and an immature need for reassurance. That reassurance can be found in God's Word and in His providential care for us.

If Miracles Are Possible Today, Why Don't We See More of Them?

Miracles come as a divine surprise. Though many miracles occurred in Bible times, remember that the Bible was written over 1,500 years and spans a time of at least 3,000 years. There were long periods of time in Bible history when no miracles were recorded. We pray for God to perform miracles. Sometimes He does, but more often He does not. Why?

I will not presume to answer the question of why we do not see more miracles, but I have a couple of thoughts. First, God in His grace knows that we would be destroyed by too many miracles.

God is the creator of the natural order. As finite creatures, we are unable to cope with an inconsistent universe. If miracles became common, life for us would become a theater of the absurd. Our sanity would not be able to withstand the frequent suspension of "normal" reality. Our expectations would be constantly raised and lowered, and moral chaos would ensue. Should we work for food or look for manna? Should we stop taking our children to the doctor? Should we quit our jobs and go sit on a mountain waiting to hear the Savior's voice? If we don't hear His voice audibly or see a visible manifestation of His glory, should we be seeking someone else who has?

There is also a potentially devastating matter of responsibility and accountability regarding miracles. Think of the many miracles God performed when He brought our people out of Egypt. Remember the short memories of our people? Remember the grumbling, the golden calf, etc.? In the days characterized by miracles, people were frequently "zapped" by God, struck dead or fatally ill. Judgment is very harsh for those who have seen such concrete evidence of God's reality and do not respond in obedience.

These reasons fit the big picture, but might sound hard-hearted when it comes to the people who just want one small miracle: the couple who have been told they can never bear children and cannot understand why their prayers for a miracle child have not been answered. Or what about the mother who prays that her terminally ill child will be healed, or the children in the Middle East, Bosnia or Rwanda who are praying that the killing will stop? We don't need a multitude of miracles, just a few here and there. Why are they so rare?

We need to realize that there is another question behind that question, and it is a big one: why does an all-powerful God allow so much suffering in the world? That is really what the person who just wants one or two miracles is asking. And we only have the answer in part. We do not know why God intervenes to alleviate some of the suffering and allows other suffering to run its "natural" course.

We do know that some of the suffering in our lives is intended as opportunity for victory—not through a miracle, but through the testing of our faith, which produces patience. By letting God see us through the suffering, our faith is strengthened and we will be complete (James 1).

We also know that God's miracles are not intended to bring heaven here to earth or to transform our problems into paradise. God's miracles point to something other and something better. He wants people to be homesick for heaven and to long for His presence instead of the world and its enticements. In order for that to happen we must know the world for what it is: a place of sin and rebellion that causes suffering for the innocent as well as the guilty.

It would be wrong to say that God enjoys allowing pain or suffering. It would be wrong to say that we fully understand why He does not prevent it. But it is right to say that God is good and that we ought to trust Him.

What Should We Believe About Miracles?

We cannot know God's purposes completely. But we can know that He has revealed himself in certain miraculous ways throughout history. He commanded us to record and recite those miracles from generation to generation. God placed certain landmark miracles in history so that we might recognize and participate in His redemptive plans, and glorify Him for accomplishing His purposes. We know that this is so in the history of the Jewish people and in the history of the early church. It will be so again when the prophecies of the Second Coming of Y'shua are fulfilled.

I believe that miracles do happen today, perhaps more often than we might know, yet not as often as many might claim. God has answered some of my prayers in such a way and at such a time that I cannot help but believe it is a miracle. Other prayers have gone unanswered—or as some might put it, have been answered in the negative. Let me illustrate what I mean.

The birth of our second child, Ilana Michelle, came after a difficult pregnancy for my wife, Patti. During her last trimester she developed sciatica, a painful condition in her leg caused by the position of the baby pressing down on a nerve. It was difficult for Patti to sleep at night, and she had to walk with a cane during the day. This condition lasted for several weeks. One night while we were at the Jews for Jesus West Coast Ingathering, she was in so much pain that she barely slept at all. The next morning, I called our then two-year-old son, Isaac, over and the two of us laid hands on Patti's leg. We prayed that God would heal her.

Without any fanfare or outward sensation, God answered our prayer. From that moment, Patti had no more pain in her leg and the condition never returned. Nevertheless several weeks later Patti developed bronchitis. Because she was still carrying the baby, there was very little medication she could take. Her coughing spasms were so violent that she strained the muscles around her ribs. She had to try to sleep sitting up to avoid the spasms. Once again, Isaac and I prayed. We asked the Lord to heal her, yet Patti continued to suffer with bronchitis. We did not doubt our God because He did not answer within the time we had hoped. Nor did we cease to be thankful for His healing her sciatica. We must not stop praising God for the wonders He has done because we are disappointed about the wonders He has not done!

When we ask ourselves if we really believe in miracles, for those of us who know the Lord the answer must be a resounding "yes!" If we have been truly born again, we have experienced the miraculous. We have been joined to the Lord of creation, who interrupted nature by His miraculous birth and conquered death by His astounding resurrection.

Beyond that, we may or may not witness a miracle in our lifetime. We should never deny the possibility of a miracle because the Almighty is not confined to our ideas of what is possible. Nor should we expect God to prove His love to us or validate our faith by suspending the laws of nature.

God reveals himself both through miracles and through the manifold acts of His providence. Somewhere between providence and miracle we find the reality of God's daily presence in our lives, and that is where we must anchor our souls. We draw strength in those times when our own efforts are exhausted and we see our heavenly Father intervene in the affairs of our lives to accomplish His purposes. This is the reality we seek: more of God, less of ourselves. Whether we see Him through providence, phenomenal answers to prayer or miracle—let's be content for Him to decide. The sign we should seek is the sign of His coming; the wonder we can experience daily is His transforming power that makes us more like Y'shua.

We Want Messiah Now!

No one on this earth has seen anything like the great and awesome day that is about to come. The world, as we know it, will come to a screeching halt. In an instant, all that matters to our daily lives will matter no more.

In my imagination it begins as a distant sound that quickly builds in volume. It is like no other sound we've ever heard. As it swells, like a resounding trumpet, growing more and more intense, it forces every man, woman and child to stop whatever he or she is doing. It is not a piercing or painful sound, but it overpowers all. It vibrates around us, within us, throughout our beings. The sound mysteriously lifts our gaze toward the sky. And as we stare, transfixed, a flash of brilliance—brighter than any atomic explosion—sears the sky. The light is not only seen but is felt. It fills our eyes, our hearts, and it's almost unbearable. Yet still we can, still we must, continue our gaze upward. Some quake in terror, while others tremble with joy.

A chorus of brilliant tones joins the brightness in the sky. And there, accompanied by an innumerable host, is our Messiah, Y'shua. Some are unprepared and cower in fear, but we stand with tears of jubilation, inwardly laughing, yet silent, in awe before the Lord of glory. As His foot touches the Mount of Olives, the temporal is instantly and irrevocably overcome by the eternal. Eternity has once again intruded to dominate history, this time, once and for all. That which was hoped for, now is. He who was longed for arrives. The earth is changed, and the glorious presence of Y'shua beckons, "Welcome, welcome my children."

Maybe you imagine it differently. The main thing is to try to imagine it *somehow* and to let it be the object of our greatest longing. While we may anticipate many events and experiences, our ultimate yearning must be for the fulfillment of that hope!

For the grace of God that brings salvation has appeared to all men, teaching us that, denying ungodliness and worldly lusts, we should live soberly, righteously, and godly in the present age, looking for the blessed hope and glorious appearing of our great God and Savior Jesus Christ, who gave Himself for us, that He might redeem us from every lawless deed and purify for Himself His own special people, zealous for good works. (Titus 2:11-14)

Y'shua and His coming are our Blessed Hope, more holy, more beautiful and in every way more worthy of our devotion than anything or anyone! The fact that we will see Him face to face should make a difference in every moment of our lives.

Still, it is a struggle to be continually aware of that reality. How often do we think or speak about the return of our Messiah—not in sanctimonious rhetoric where we can recognize each other by pious shibboleths—but with genuine, honest discussions about our Hope of Hopes?

Do you find yourself frequently more motivated by the pressing business of today than by the Blessed Hope? Most Jewish believers in Jesus the Messiah believe in His literal, physical return. Yet we sometimes lose the immediacy of that hope amidst a crush of "priorities." Perhaps at times, thoughts of His return do not stir up great joy, but churn up uneasiness because we would not like to face our Lord at that particular moment.

We should use that uneasiness to identify and deal with whatever prevents us from wanting to face the Lord. It's a signal for us to repent, make restitution or take whatever action is appropriate. Nevertheless it's easy to dismiss that uneasiness on the grounds that we are not likely to be facing Him any time soon. Which raises the question:

Do We Really Believe Jesus Could Come at Any Time?

The teaching that Jesus could return at any moment is known as the doctrine of imminence. Some believers in Jesus have neglected that doctrine because they interpret the Bible to mean that certain things must occur in a particular sequence before Y'shua returns.

This chapter is not about the apocalyptic events preceding the return of Messiah or the many opinions expounded on that subject. But the two expectations can run to two extremes. There are kingdom builders who feel that we will accomplish all things that are needful before the Messiah is to return. They believe we will have all things lined up "in a row" including personal right-eousness, then the Lord will come. Others have despaired of doing anything to help make the world a better place. They only hope that at any moment Y'shua will return to rescue them from this toxic, noxious planet.

Could the Messiah come at any time, or is He constrained by a chain of events that have not yet occurred? Should we do all we can to hasten His coming or should we do nothing at all, knowing that all efforts are in vain?

According to Jewish tradition, there is the account of one Rabbi Zera who, "whenever he chanced upon scholars engaged [in calculating the time of the Messiah's coming], he would say to them: 'I beg of you, do not postpone it, for it has been taught: Three come unawares: Messiah, a found article and a scorpion'" (Sanhedrin 97a). Which means, since the Messiah only comes when unexpected, don't keep Him away with your calculations!

Yet in another place we are told, "If Israel repents for one day, forthwith the son of David will come. . . . If Israel would keep a single Sabbath in the proper way, forthwith the son of David will come" (Jerusalem Talmud, Ta'anit 1:1).[1]

What do you think when you see Jewish newspapers filled with *Chabad*[2] ads and columns urging people to bring the Messiah quickly through the doing of *mitzvot*?[3] It is painful, is it not, to think that some people seem to regard the Almighty as though He were harnessed by some kind of a cosmic tether, and if we pull hard enough on our end, He will be forced to move.

Yet, many in Jesus have determined to do what they believe is necessary to usher in God's reign. For example, in the field of evangelism and world mission, there has been heady talk of "a church for every people and the gospel for every person by A.D. 2000." This is a lofty goal, but why not 1998 or 2004? Is there

---

1. Jacob Neusner, *Messiah in Context* (Philadelphia: Fortress Press, 1984), p. 122.

2. *Chabad:* an organization of ultra-Orthodox followers of the Lubavitch rabbi; the word Chabad is an acronym for three Hebrew words that are translated wisdom, reason and intuition.

3. *Mitzvot:* good deeds that fulfill the commands and observances of the Law by which Jewish people seek to gain merit with God.

something special about the start of a new millennium?

In his book *Operation World* Patrick Johnstone assembled a mind-numbing array of statistics to demonstrate that we are 75 to 85 percent of the way toward finishing the task of evangelizing the world. He declares: "Jesus gave the promise in Matthew 24:14 that when this task was accomplished, the end would come" (page 26).

Many appreciate the incentive proposed by this notion. Nevertheless, our commitment to evangelize the world should be based on love and obedience to the Lord's command, not on the hope that we can hasten the end. Scripture does not offer world evangelism as the Blessed Hope, nor as the means to bring about the Blessed Hope. And what of those of us who are Jewish believers? We may not talk about world evangelization, but some talk of being the instrument of an end-time messianic Jewish revival.

You might think it unlikely that anyone would actually believe we are proclaiming the gospel in order to hasten the return of Y'shua. Yet several leading figures in the mainstream Jewish community, and even some not-so-leading figures, have concluded that the motivation for evangelism is a Christian belief that Jesus cannot return until the Jewish people believe in Him. "Christians believe the messiah will come in the year 2000, but only if all Jews accept Jesus as the messiah," quoted Tovia Singer in an article by Steve Feldman for *The Jewish Exponent* in Philadelphia, Pennsylvania (July 1, 1993).

Likewise, some of our unbelieving brethren explain Christian support of Israel in a similar way. Perhaps they have seen the same advertisement I saw in a major Christian magazine: "Why just read about end-times prophecy? Help make it happen." The ad went on to request donations for helping Russian Jews go to Israel.

What is most troubling is that many groups involved in endeavors to "help fulfill prophecy" have promised the Israeli government that they will not tell our people about Jesus! They justify these agreements by saying that God will bring our people to the Lord in the Land of Israel, and not outside of the Land. They are trying to fulfill prophecy, which is God's business, while neglecting the Great Commission, which is not only their business, but also the duty of every believer. People in every land are dying without Christ, separated from God forever, no matter what country they were in when they died.

I believe God's promise to bring Jewish people back to the Land, and it is exciting to think that the establishment of today's State of Israel could be part of the fulfillment of promise. I cannot be certain of this, and I don't think any of us can. Scripture seems to leave room for debate and discussion concerning what God is doing with the nation of Israel and the Jewish people's return. We *can* say with certainty that nowhere do the Scriptures teach that the return of Jewish people to the Land is a necessary prelude to the Messiah's return. I believe that it could have been possible for Y'shua to return prior to 1948. Furthermore, I believe that Y'shua could just as easily return tomorrow morning while the majority of the Jewish people are still outside of the Land.

I believe that one way or another, all Jews will be in Israel some day. But the greatest hope that we proclaim must be our Blessed Hope, the return of Y'shua. As followers of the Messiah Y'shua, we should know and believe that those things the world hopes for will never satisfy us. We say with the psalmist, "And now, Lord, what do I wait for? My hope is in You" (Psalm 39:7).

Our hope must always be in what God can do, not in what we can do. Still we want to obey those things He commanded: to love one another, to tell the lost the good news of Jesus, to make disciples. We can do these things moment by moment, day by day as we anticipate His return.

It is easy to lose sight of the things we want Him to find us doing in that moment when His foot sets down on the Mount of Olives.

It is all too easy to busy ourselves with the good things, but not the right things. That tendency is compounded when we allow ourselves to think that this and that must happen before the Lord returns; therefore, we have plenty of time. When we think we have plenty of time, we usually don't use time as well as we could.

For example, many Christian groups place major emphases on

church growth. There are church growth seminars, institutes for church growth and articles on how to grow churches. It is right to want to see people added to the church, but in some cases we end up with a Christianity that emphasizes the church and not the Christ. Some call this "Churchianity." Whatever it is, it puts people in danger of making the church, rather than Jesus, their hope. We in the community of Jewish believers may not always use the term *church growth,* but some overemphasize the growth of Messianic Jewish congregations, which is the same thing.

I am certain that some day all Israel will know the Messiah Jesus, but it won't be through the expansion of congregations. It will be brought about by the outpouring of the Holy Spirit prophesied in Zechariah 12:10. Our people will look upon Y'shua and recognize who He is, who He always has been and who He always will be. It will be a time of mourning, repentance, return and joy through tears.

It will be a time worthy of all the mention God gives it in Scriptures. There are 7,959 verses in the New Testament, 330 of which refer to the Second Coming. That is one out of every 25 verses. Y'shua referred to His return 21 times, and there are more than 50 exhortations in Scripture urging us to be ready for that event!

The Hebrew Scriptures also set forth numerous messianic prophecies that will be fulfilled when Y'shua returns.

I put together a short list of reasons to focus on the Second Coming. You might want to list your own, using different Scriptures to highlight other aspects of the Blessed Hope. My list is as follows:

1. The Blessed Hope is motivation to godly living.

The thought that Jesus could come at any time sets us in motion. We want to feel that at any moment, our overriding response to His appearing would be joy. The thought of His imminent return should keep us continually confessing and repenting of our sin.

> Beloved, now we are children of God; and it has not yet been revealed what we shall be, but we know that when He is revealed, we shall be like Him, for we shall see Him as

He is. And everyone who has this hope in Him purifies himself, just as He is pure. (1 John 3:2-3)

2. The Blessed Hope is a means to establish God's justice.

In a world rife with injustice, it is a blessing to anticipate the day when God will deliver His people. In that day, righteousness will not be mocked and wickedness will not be exalted.

> There shall be a time of trouble, such as never was since there was a nation, even to that time. And at that time your people shall be delivered, every one who is found written in the book. And many of those who sleep in the dust of the earth shall awake, some to everlasting life, some to shame and everlasting contempt. Those who are wise shall shine like the brightness of the firmament, and those who turn many to righteousness like the stars forever and ever. (Daniel 12:1-3)

3. The Blessed Hope is memorialized in our worship.

It is important to obey Y'shua by remembering together the words He pronounced:

> The Lord Jesus on the same night in which He was betrayed took bread; and when He had given thanks, He broke it and said, "Take, eat; this is My body which is broken for you; do this in remembrance of Me." In the same manner He also took the cup after supper, saying, "This cup is the new covenant in My blood. This do, as often as you drink it, in remembrance of Me." For as often as you eat this bread and drink this cup, you proclaim the Lord's death till He comes. (1 Corinthians 11:23-26)

4. The Blessed Hope is the moment we meet the Lord—and are reunited with those we love in the Lord.

God has promised that we shall meet Him! As if that weren't enough, we will also be reunited with those from whom death has temporarily separated us. This is hope in its fullest meaning!

> But I do not want you to be ignorant, brethren, concerning those who have fallen asleep, lest you sorrow as others

who have no hope. For if we believe that Jesus died and rose again, even so God will bring with Him those who sleep in Jesus. For this we say to you by the word of the Lord, that we who are alive and remain until the coming of the Lord will by no means precede those who are asleep. For the Lord Himself will descend from heaven with a shout, with the voice of an archangel, and with the trumpet of God. And the dead in Christ will rise first. Then we who are alive and remain shall be caught up together with them in the clouds to meet the Lord in the air. And thus we shall always be with the Lord. Therefore comfort one another with these words. (1 Thessalonians 4:13-18)

Those are just a few examples—God's Word says so much more about the Blessed Hope. If you take the time to meditate on these and other passages that describe the return of Y'shua, you will be blessed. But be prepared for a shift in priorities!

If we have the Blessed Hope, we are not going to be building cathedrals. Some of us might begin to look at 30-year mortgages and wonder about beating the lender out of a few payments! We should not live without any thought for the future, but we have to live in the light of the immediate future, not the far future.

What is the best thing that can happen to you tomorrow? Win the lottery? Have an erring mate return? Find out that your son or daughter won a full scholarship to Harvard, Yale or some other Ivy League school? Maybe you could discover the fountain of youth and be ten years younger after a dip? Whatever might capture your imagination must pale in comparison to the thought of being in the presence of the God Who chose to dwell among us.

My grandfather, Fred Kendall, was a believer in Jesus, and one of the last things he told me before he died was, "David, I'm not waiting for the undertaker. I'm looking for the uppertaker!" I want to be like that. I want to be counted among those "who have loved His appearing" (2 Timothy 4:8). Our hope, that which we set our hearts on, should be His appearing—and it should also be our message to others. Jesus is coming!

What other message enables us to shine so much hope in a world of hopelessness, to radiate truth in a world where false hopes lead so many astray?

Therefore, let us strive to seek the Lord, to stand firm in the Lord, to serve the Lord with gladness, knowing that we just might be in His glorious presence tonight or tomorrow morning. Let Him be our all in all, above all, beyond all. Then thoughts of His return will never be far from our consciousness, stirring our hearts to experience every ounce of joy that God created us to have in Him.

Lord, Y'shua, be our all until You gather us all to Yourself. Maranatha!

Afterword: For Our Gentile Family in Christ

You have been reading messages originally written to the family of Jewish believers in Jesus. Whether you are Jewish or Gentile, I hope that you have found that what we have to say to one another speaks to all who love Israel's Messiah.

I have also included a message written specifically to the rest of our mishpochah, to those of you who are not Jewish. You see, there would be no messages to Jewish believers in Jesus if it were not for friends such as you—because there would be no Jewish believers to read them! Without caring Christians who are bold enough to witness to their unsaved Jewish friends and neighbors, without generous friends to help us reach out to our own, the family of Jewish believers would indeed be minuscule. (As it is, we're just tiny!)

We need you to care about Jewish evangelism, and we need you to help other Christians care. Has Paul's admonition that the gospel should go "to the Jew first" ever puzzled you or struck you as a somewhat unfair display of favoritism? Then perhaps the following will shed some light on what it means to be chosen . . . and how your choice to make Jewish evangelism one of your Christian concerns can go a long way in spreading the good news of Jesus.

To the Jew First

"God, they say we are the chosen people," remarks Tevye, a Jewish character in the play *Fiddler on the Roof.* "For once, God, couldn't you choose somebody else?"

Tevye's sentiment reflects an ambivalence common among today's Jews. That reluctance to embrace all it means to be chosen may be understandable in a people who have suffered so much persecution over the centuries. More puzzling, however, is the ambivalence of many Christians toward Jews.

Still the Chosen People

While it's true that the Jewish people haven't been a light to the nations as God commanded them to be, God still has a plan

for His people Israel. The Apostle Paul declared about the chosenness of the Jewish people, "the gifts and the calling of God are
irrevocable" (Romans 11:29). As Paul pointed out in Romans 11,
God wants to graft His chosen people back onto the rich root of
the Olive Tree. He wants Jewish people to come to know *Y'shua*
(Hebrew for Jesus), their Messiah and the Savior of the world.

"Now if their fall is riches for the world, and their failure
riches for the Gentiles, how much more their fullness!" Paul
wrote (Romans 11:12). The Bible is clear that reaching the
Jewish people with the gospel is a key part of God's plan for the
salvation of the whole world. Jewish evangelism is the starting
point for the Great Commission.

The strategy of the modern missions movement is flawed
because it has failed to properly consider this special concern.
The Apostle Paul stated that the gospel is "to the Jew first," but
some missiologists prefer to see this a statement of historical past
rather than a priority guide for a continuing mission strategy. As
a result, when it comes to reaching Jews, the Great Commission
has developed a Great Omission.

A Biblical Primacy

Today's missiologists often develop mission strategies based
on sociological factors. But missiology should be an interdisci-
plinary study between theology and the social sciences.

Certainly it makes sense for missions to glean some insight
from sociology and anthropology—but all too often these
disciplines take precedence over scriptural mandates. Many
missiologists have limited the role of theology to a matter of
establishing the imperatives. They allow the Bible to say why it's
important to go into all the world and preach the gospel, but they
often don't consult it concerning the manner in which to proceed.

Just as there is a biblical reason to go, there is a biblical way
to perform the task. God has given us the formula. So why are
we looking around to see who needs the gospel most in order to
determine how we evangelize? The Samaritan wasn't on his way
to Jericho to find out who needed his services!

It is not enough to say that the largest percentage of unreached
people is in one geographic location or among one particular

ethnic or religious entity. These and similar strategies presume that people and place are the same.

As Dr. Paul Pierson, dean emeritus of Fuller School of World Mission, has pointed out, the internationalization and urbanization of world populations means that we can no longer limit our strategies to location. We must be prepared to reach Cambodians in Los Angeles, Muslims in London and so on. Further, he notes, the great spiritual movements more often began on the periphery of a society rather than with the majority. Demographics are not the best tools for determining missions strategy.

The Bible actually has much to say about missions methodology. And as we study Scripture, we can't avoid the primacy of the Jewish people in God's strategy.

If we look at the 10/40 Window (an area between a specific latitude and longitude that many feel should be a focus for evangelism), Israel is right in the middle. So the 10/40 Window approach should properly include Jewish evangelism. But focusing on Israel, the place, in one's strategy for evangelizing Jews is a mistake. Israel is not just a place; Israel is a people.

Finally Fruitful

The church may have neglected to take the gospel to the Jews in modern times because it has viewed Jewish evangelism as a fruitless endeavor. It's not fruitless anymore.

The Jews are a universal people, and the majority of them live outside the land of Israel. God is at work among them today in a marvelous way—especially in countries other than Israel.

The greatest evidence of God's work among the Jews today can be seen in the former Soviet Union, where nearly one million Jews live. Avi Snyder, station chief for Jews for Jesus in Moscow, reports a remarkable openness to the gospel among Russian Jews. In the five years that the organization's missionaries have been working there, 1,324 Russian Jews have received Jesus as their Savior and Lord. Similar reports have come from other mission groups working in former Soviet states.

This openness is not limited to the former Soviet Union. With half the world's Jewish population living within its borders, the United States is also fertile ground for Jewish evangelism.

The formation of messianic congregations—gatherings of Jewish and Gentile Christians into local worshiping communities—is further evidence that God is at work among the Jewish people today. While most of these congregations are small, they can still be viewed in part as a result of effective evangelism among Jews in America.

Not all of this evangelism has been carried out by mission or evangelistic organizations. Individual Christians from a wide variety of backgrounds have been instrumental in sharing the gospel with their family members, neighbors and acquaintances.

We Need to Witness

A myth prevails that Gentile Christians cannot effectively reach out to their Jewish friends. However, with just a little instruction about Jewish sensitivities, most Christians can have very effective testimonies to Jewish people. In fact, in surveys conducted by Jews for Jesus most of the Jewish Christians polled reported they were led to Christ by a Gentile friend.

There is no doubt that Jewish people are tougher to share the gospel with than many other people. They may be just as difficult to lead to the Lord as Muslims. If you can witness to Jews, you can witness to just about anybody. And with the Holy Spirit's help, you *can* witness to Jews.

Witnessing to Jewish people in our own communities is the first of two important roles that Christians have to play in Jewish missions. The second is that Gentile believers need to follow the biblical mandate to "pray for the peace of Jerusalem."

We Need to Pray

The only way peace can come to Jerusalem is through the Prince of Peace, Jesus the Messiah. Christians must devote themselves to pray for the salvation of the Jewish people and for the work of Jewish evangelism as it is carried out around the world.

Praying for and giving to Jewish missions may seem obvious responsibilities for Christians in general, yet the majority of evangelical believers and churches do not actively support missions to the Jews or specifically pray for the salvation of Jewish people. We are thankful for the exceptions; nevertheless, even among those who do support Jewish missions, we find some who do so as more of an afterthought than a strategic commitment.

If we want to restore biblical strategy to the mission of the church, this must change.

Getting Started

Hudson Taylor, who founded the China Inland Mission, had a tradition for starting each year. Every New Year's Day, he sent a check to the Mildmay Mission to the Jews in London. On each check he wrote, "To the Jew first."

Simultaneously, John Wilkinson, leader of the Mildmay Mission, sent his personal check to the China Inland Mission with the notation, "And also to the Gentile."

These two great nineteenth-century missionaries recognized something that today's church must remember. The Jewish people are still God's chosen people. They must be our starting point for fulfilling the Great Commission.

Much material is available to help Christians in witnessing to Jews. One good source for such material is the Messianic Resource Catalog *(available through Purple Pomegranate Productions, 80 Page Street, San Francisco, CA 94102).*

THE JEWS FOR JESUS ORGANIZATION was founded in September of 1973 to proclaim the message of the Messiah to all people. Moishe Rosen, a veteran missionary to the Jewish people, was the founding executive director. He committed himself to creative forms of communication to point people to Jesus, and that became a benchmark of Jews for Jesus.

We are evangelists and see ourselves as an arm of the local church. We don't feel our work with a new believer is complete until he or she takes an active role in a local, New Testament congregation.

We have full-time staff members in locations throughout the United States and around the world—all supported solely through the contributions of individuals and churches. We are raising the gospel banner from Los Angeles to New York City, from London to Johannesburg, from Moscow to Tel Aviv. We also have dozens of co-laborers in Messiah who carry out various aspects of the ministry on a volunteer basis.

We do our best to go anywhere, anytime, by any means possible to bring the message of Messiah to those who want to hear it. Many of the Jewish people we are able to help are referred to us by Christian friends such as you.

If you would like to receive our free monthly newsletter, or if you have Jewish friends you would like us to witness to, please write to us at 60 Haight Street, San Francisco, CA 94102-5895 or call us at (415) 864-2600. You can reach us electronically at one of two addresses: jfj@jews-for-jesus.org or our home page on the world wide web: htpp://www.jews-for-jesus.org.